Battleground: Wars of the Roses

BARNET 1471

Death of a Kingmaker

With the continued expansion of the Battleground Series a **Battleground Series Club** has been formed to benefit the reader. The purpose of the Club is to keep members informed of new titles and to offer many other reader-benefits. Membership is free and by registering an interest you can help us predict print runs and thus assist us in maintaining the quality and prices at their present levels.

Please call the office on 01226 734555, or send your name and address along with a request for more information to:

Battleground Series Club Pen & Sword Books Ltd,
47 Church Street, Barnsley, South Yorkshire S70 2AS

Battleground: Wars of the Roses

BARNET 1471

Death of a Kingmaker

DAVID CLARK

Pen & Sword
MILITARY

First published in Great Britain in 2007 by
Pen & Sword Military
an imprint of
Pen & Sword Books Ltd
47 Church Street
Barnsley
South Yorkshire
S70 2AS

ISBN 1-84415-236-7

Typeset in Century Old Style

Printed and bound in Great Britain by CPI UK

The Publishers would like to thank Geoffrey Wheeler for all the assistance he
has given to them in the preparation of the illustrations for this book.

For a complete list of Pen & Sword titles, please contact
Pen & Sword Books Limited
47 Church Street, Barnsley, South Yorkshire, S70 2AS, England
E-mail: enquiries@pen-and-sword.co.uk
Website: www.pen-and-sword.co.uk

Contents

Introduction

BATTLEFIELDS OF THE
WARS OF THE ROSES

D ESPITE MUCH RAISING OF AWARENESS, British battlefields are still an endangered species, continually threatened by the creeping sickness of housing developments, ubiquitous industrial estates and, more recently, sprawling dual-carriageways. Major casualties of the latter epidemic include the English Civil War battlefields of Newbury (1643) and Naseby (1645), and the Jacobite battlefield of Killiecrankie (1689).

In terms of survival, the battlefields of the Wars of the Roses (1455-1487) have fared quite well, despite five and a half centuries of 'progress' having taken their toll of essentially urban locations. Not all of the desecration is modern. The Victorians, for example, were pestilent innovators and, as early as 1852, Richard Brooke (*Visits to Fields of Battle in England of the Fifteenth Century*) could write of the Battle of Wakefield: 'There are now no traces of Wakefield Green: all of it has been enclosed, and several portions of it are built upon.' Similarly, in 1896, C.R.B. Barrett (*Battles and Battlefields in England*) wrote of the difficulties he experienced in drawing battle plans, referring to instances in which 'the topography of a place has been so changed by the hand of man as to render sketching impossible'.

Alternatively, a growing appreciation of the value of battlefields as source material for the historian is exemplified in the provision of visitor centres and on-site battle plans – as at Wakefield and Towton respectively. Perhaps the real threat to Wars of the Roses battlefields lies in their historical remoteness. In the popular imagination, the Wars of the Roses have retreated into the Dark Ages. Long eclipsed by a series of more significant global conflicts, they seem to many of us as distant as the Norman Conquest. All that remains are passing references in Shakespeare, and perhaps a cursory acquaintance with the mystery of the Princes in the Tower.

Right: Map of major battlefields of the Wars of the Roses, from Hilaire Bello *Warfare in England. Best known today as the author of ferociously amusi* *verses for children, Belloc was also a respected historian and* Warfare in Engla *remains an excellent introduction to its subject.*

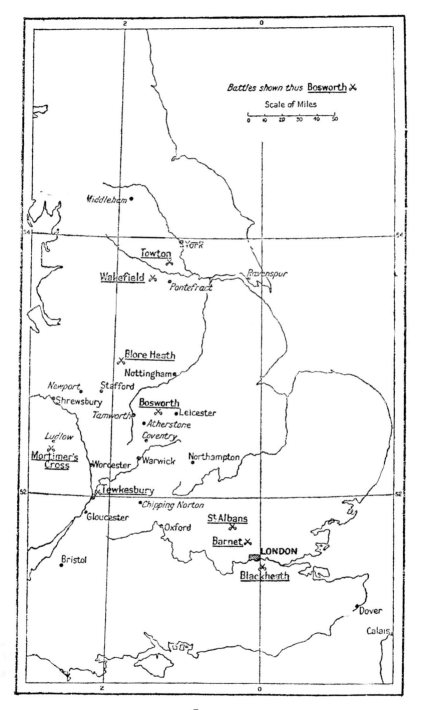

Battles shown thus <u>Bosworth</u> ✗

Scale of Miles

0 10 20 30 40 50

Middleham •

York
<u>Towton</u>
✗

<u>Wakefield</u> ✗
Pontefract •

Ravenspur

<u>Blore Heath</u>
✗
• Nottingham
Newport •   • Stafford
• Shrewsbury
Tamworth   <u>Bosworth</u>
✗   • Leicester
• Atherstone
Ludlow   • Coventry
✗
<u>Mortimer's</u>   Worcester •   • Warwick   • Northampton
<u>Cross</u>
✗ <u>Tewkesbury</u>
• Chipping Norton
• Gloucester   <u>St Albans</u>
✗ Oxford   ✗
<u>Barnet</u> ✗
LONDON
✗
<u>Blackheath</u>

• Dover

Calais

The study of Wars of the Roses battle sites is important, therefore, not only in order to help preserve the sites themselves, but as a means of keeping in touch with a momentous period in English history.

In all, there are seventeen major 'Roses' sites, viz:

St Albans (22 May 1455) (Y) Fought in the old town of St Albans, to the north of the Cathedral.

Blore Heath (23 September 1459) (Y) Two and a half miles to the east of Market Drayton. Battlefield monument.

Ludford Bridge (13 October 1459) (L) Adjoining Ludlow.

Northampton (10 July 1460) (Y) The fighting was focused on Northampton Castle, levelled in 1879 to facilitate expansion of the railway station. Only the Postern Gate remains, built into the wall by the station entrance. At the time of writing (2006), there are plans to demolish even this surviving fragment. Towards the end of the twentieth century, the southern approaches to the battlefield via Hunsbury Hill disappeared beneath a housing development.

Wakefield (30 December 1460) (L) The battle was fought to the south of Wakefield at Kirk Sandall, the site of the Norman castle – long since reduced to fragments of masonry. The landscape to the east is urbanized, but portions of the battlefield to the north and

The battlefield of Towton. Thi the largest battle of the Wars the Roses, was fought on Pal Sunday, 1461. As at Barnet, t weather was an important factor in the outcome. On thi occasion the packed Lancastrian ranks were blinded by driving snow.

west remain open. Visitor centre.

Mortimer's Cross (2 February 1461) (Y) Five miles to the north-west of Leominster. Battlefield monument.

St Albans (17 February 1461) (L) The Second Battle of St Albans was fought to the north of the old town between Barnard's Heath and Sandridge.

Ferrybridge (27–28 March 1461) (Y) Prelude to Battle of Towton, focused on the bridge over the River Aire.

Towton (29 March 1461) (Y) Three miles to the south of Tadcaster. Battlefield monument.

Hedgeley Moor (25 April 1464) (Y) Six miles to the south-east of Wooler. Battlefield monument.

Hexham (15 May 1464) (Y) Two miles to the south-east of Hexham.

Edgcote (26 July 1469) (L) Six miles to the north-east of Banbury. Precise location uncertain.

Empingham (12 March 1470) (Y) Straddling the present-day course of the A1, five miles to the north of Stamford.

Barnet (14 April 1471) (Y) Ten miles to the north of London. Battlefield monument.

Tewkesbury (4 May 1471) (Y) Precise location uncertain. Probably to the south of the town, around 'Margaret's Camp'. Battlefield monument.

Bosworth (22 August 1485) (L) Precise location uncertain. Probably two miles to the south of Market Bosworth. Visitor centre.

Stoke Field (16 June 1487) (L) Three miles to the south of Newark. Battlefield monument.

Simple arithmetic shows that the White Rose of York (Y) enjoyed a greater number of victories, but Henry Tudor, representing the Red Rose of Lancaster (L), struck what we now recognize to be the final blows at Bosworth and Stoke Field. Occasionally, two further encounters are added to the tally. On 17 June 1497 Henry VII put down a rebellion (against his taxation policy) at Blackheath; and a little later in the same year, between 17 and 18 September, the Yorkist pretender Perkin Warbeck, accompanied by 8,000 rebels, attacked Exeter but was repelled.

Only one of the major battlefield sites (Northampton) has disappeared entirely, although several (Blore Heath, Mortimer's Cross, Towton, Hedgeley Moor, Hexham, Edgcote, Empingham, Bosworth and Stoke Field) owe their preservation entirely to their rural settings. In the case of St Albans, enough of the medieval street pattern has survived to enable us to follow the course of both 'Roses' battles which occurred here.

The Battle of Barnet

The battles which initially appeared to have settled the issue in favour of the House of York are those which occupy the semi-urban locations of Barnet and Tewkesbury. Although Barnet is generally served up as an aperitif to the main course of the more celebrated Tewkesbury, the former is the more intriguing.

In the first place, it is remarkable that a site only ten miles from the centre of London has not been entirely built over. The development – including a golf course – which has taken place is of a nature which has tended to preserve rather than obliterate the open landscape. Secondly, the location itself, identified by contemporary records, is fairly accurate. This contrasts with the difficulties of fixing the location of Tewkesbury, a battle fought only three weeks later, and Bosworth, a problem for the solution of which a National Lottery grant of £1,000,000 has recently (2005) been awarded. Finally, the sources which pinpoint the site for us also provide invaluable intelligence about the course of the battle and the events leading up to it.

In addition, the battle itself provides an opportunity to examine the reputations of two of its leading participants, the Earl of Warwick and Richard, Duke of Gloucester. Was Warwick really the master tactician of legend, and are there any hints of the villainous Richard III in the conduct of the youthful Gloucester?

On a more prosaic level, Barnet is an ideal site for the battlefield explorer. Apart from enjoying the distinction of being the only battlefield in Britain which can be reached by London Underground, it is a compact, accessible site that readily lends itself to exploration, which in turn renders it an appropriate subject for the 'Battleground Britain' series.

Compact though the battlefield may be, wider consideration of the campaign necessarily involves intimacy with a broad topography. From his landing on the Yorkshire coast, at Ravenspur, on 14 March 1471, Edward IV progressed via Beverley to York. From there, he advanced south to Doncaster, Nottingham and Leicester. On 29 March he was at Coventry, from where he marched, via Daventry, Northampton, Dunstable and St Albans, to London. What were his experiences at each of these towns, and how did they help to shape the course of the battle to come? A meaningful study of any battle demands far more than a description of the action itself, occurring over a short period of time in a few acres of ground, and the Battle of Barnet is no exception.

Plan of the Book

Of necessity, books about Wars of the Roses battles are invariably prefaced by background information on the thirty-year conflict. This one is no exception, although each section is 'self-contained', allowing the narrative to commence at what is an appropriate point for the individual reader.

There follows an account of the campaign, from the date of the exiled Edward's arrival on the Yorkshire coast, through the marches of both factions via the Midlands to the battlefield itself. A full account of the battle is followed by an examination of its repercussions.

Central to the book is a fully illustrated guided tour of the battlefield – enabling visitors to follow the course of the action step-by-step.

Additional features include a presentation of the folklore and traditions associated with the topic, a discussion of the arms and armour used in the battle and a review of major contemporary and modern source material, together with guidance for further reading.

Timeline: The Wars of the Roses in Context

1441 Eton College founded.
1450 Jack Cade's Rebellion.
1450 Johannes Gutenberg invents the printing press.
1451 Glasgow University founded.
1453 End of Hundred Years' War.
1455 First Battle of St Albans.
1456 Magdalen College, Oxford, founded.
1459 Battle of Blore Heath.
1459 Battle of Ludford Bridge.
1460 Battle of Northampton.
1460 Battle of Wakefield.
1461 France introduces a postal service.
1461 Battle of Mortimer's Cross.
1461 Second Battle of St Albans.
1461 Turks conquer Greece.
1461 Battle of Ferrybridge.
1461 Battle of Towton.
1464 Battle of Hedgeley Moor.
1464 Battle of Hexham.
1469 Battle of Edgcote.
1470 Battle of Empingham.
1471 Battle of Barnet.
1471 Battle of Tewkesbury.
1471 Pliny establishes first European observatory.
1471 Sir Thomas Malory completes *Morte d'Arthur*.
1477 William Caxton produces first printed book in England.
1478 Spanish Inquisition established.
1479 Plague in England.
1485 Battle of Bosworth.
1485 Botticelli paints 'The Birth of Venus'.
1487 Battle of Stoke Field.
1488 James III of Scotland murdered.
1492 Christopher Columbus discovers West Indies.
1497 John Cabot discovers Newfoundland.
1499 Perkin Warbeck executed.

Chapter One

CONTEMPORARY SOURCES

T HERE ARE ABOUT A DOZEN major contemporary or near-contemporary sources of information about the Battle of Barnet. *The Historie of the Arrivall of Edward IV* is still regarded as the definitive contemporary account. Unashamedly Yorkist in sentiment, the anonymous author describes Edward's almost single-handed destruction of his foes:

> *...for the Kynge, trusing verely in God's helpe, owr blessyd ladyes, and Seynt George, toke to hym great haries and corage for to supprese the falcehode of all them that so falcely and so traytorowsly had conspired agaynst hym, wherethrwghe, with the faylhefull, wellbelovyd, and mayghty assystaunce of his felawshipe, that in great nombar deseveryd nat from his parson, and were as well assvred unto hym, as to them was possyble, he mannly, vigorowsly, and valliantly assayled them, in the mydst and strongest of theyr battaile, where he, with great violence, bett and bare down afore hym all that stode in hys way, and, than, turned to the range, first on that one hand, and than on that othar hand, in lengthe, and so bet and bate them downe, so that nothing myght stande in the syght of hym.*

John Warkworth, Master of Peterhouse College, Cambridge, produced his *First 13 Years of the Reign of Edward IV* in 1483. Although his sympathies were with the House of Lancaster, he provides an objective account of the battle. According to Warkworth, Edward was first on the scene at Barnet:

> *But it happenede that he withe his oste were entrede into the toune of Barnet, before the Erle of Warwyke and his oste. And so the Erle of Warwyke and his oste lay witheoute the toune alle nyght, and eche of them loosede gonnes at othere, alle the nyghte.*

Polydore Vergil, a papal tax collector who decided to settle in England, wrote his *Anglica Historia* at the behest of Henry VII.

Above: A contemporary portrait of Edward IV.

Opposite: Edward IV as depicted in John Rastell's Pastime of the People, *illustrated with the author's own rough woodcuts and published in 1529. A lawyer and MP, Rastell may have spoken with descendants of men who had fought at Barnet.*

Upon his own admission, Vergil spent six years in reading and sought out 'every man of age who was pointed out to me as having been formerly occupied in important and public affairs'. Notwithstanding his alleged objectivity, the tone of his writing clearly shows his desire to please his master – even to the extent of

The Paston Letters

The Paston family of Caister Castle in Norfolk provided a unique insight into fifteenth-century life through the miraculous survival of their personal letters, many of which were written by Margaret Paston to her husband, John, a lawyer who spent much of his time on business in London.

One of the most interesting features of the correspondence is its essentially mundane content, with Margaret writing about the day to day problems of managing the estate in her husband's absence – proof that during this most turbulent period of history, the world still turned and life went on. Inevitably, however, the Pastons were drawn in to the Wars of the Roses.

In this respect, the letters illustrate the ease with which a family could change sides. Initially, John Paston was a loyal subject of Henry VI. When Edward IV took over, John transferred his allegiance. John died in 1466 and his sons, John Paston II and John Paston III threw in their lot with the Earl of Warwick, who they saw as a potential saviour in a long-running feud with the Duke of Norfolk.

Caister Castle had belonged to Sir John Fastolff – the model for Shakespeare's Falstaff. Years of legal wrangling resulted from Fastolff's will, with the Pastons and Fastolff's heirs both claiming ownership. The heirs sold their alleged rights to the Yorkist Duke of Norfolk who took possession of the castle in 1469, following an armed siege. So it came to pass that John II and John III fought with Warwick at the Battle of Barnet.

When news of the outcome reached Margaret, she was frantic with worry, amid rumours that both her sons had been killed. Thankfully, four days after the battle the elder John wrote to his mother to tell her that, although he and his brother were safe, they were desperately short of funds. Further, John III was 'hurte wyth an arow on his ryght arme', although he had benefited from the attentions of 'a sorion whyche [who] hathe dressid hym'. Recuperating, John III also wrote to Margaret, begging for aid as 'by my trowth my lechecrafte and fesyk, and rewardys to them that haue kept me and condyt me to London, hathe cost me sythe Estern Day more than v li. And now I haue neythr met, drink, clothys, lechecraft, nor money but vu-on borowying.'

John II was soon pardoned by Edward IV, but John III had to wait until July 1471, when he was able to advise Margaret that 'Syr Thomas Wyngffeld sent to me and let me wet that the Kyng had syngnyd my bylle of perdon, whyche the seyd Syr Thomas delyueryd me; and so by Fryday at the forthest I tryst to haue my perdon ensealyd by the Chanceler.'

The family had been fortunate. Ultimately, they transferred their allegiance to Henry VII, and in 1487 John Paston III fought alongside Henry at the Battle of Stoke, where he was knighted for his services to his new master.

The ruins of Caister Castle, home of the Paston Family.

his failure to acknowledge the presence at Barnet of the future Richard III.

The Great Chronicle of London, the author of which may have been Robert Fabian, a London merchant, is concerned primarily with the history of the capital. Thus the situation in London immediately before the battle is dealt with in some detail.

Edward Halle, a barrister, published *The Union of the Two Noble and Illustre Famelies of Lancastre and Yorke* in 1548. Much used as a source by Shakespeare, Halle ascribes a glorious death to both Warwick and Montagu:

> *But when his souldiers beyng sore wounded, weried with so long a conflict, did geve litle regarde to his wordes, he beyng a manne of a mynde invincible, rushed into the middest of his enemies, where as he (aventured so farre from his awne compagnie, to kil and sley his adversaries, that he could not be rescued) was in the middes of his enemies, striken doune and slain. The marque Montacute, thinkyng to succor his brother, whiche he*

sawe was in greate ieoperdy, and yet in hope to obtein the victory, was likewise over throwen and slain.

The *Chronicle of the Abbey of Crowland* was compiled by the members of the Abbey community. The author of the period which takes in the Battle of Barnet was, for a time, in the employ of Edward IV. Thus, the tenor is unashamedly Yorkist.

Of the minor sources, the Paston Letters are the most tantalizing. Here, we have two brothers who actually fought at Barnet. Add to this the penchant of the Pastons for letter writing, mix thoroughly, and the result should be a detailed account of the battle. Instead, only the occasional fragment is present in the surviving correspondence, although the family does display its Lancastrian leanings in continuing expressions of concern for the welfare of Queen Margaret of Anjou:

> *As for othere tythynges is understande here that the Qwyen Margrett is verrely londyd, and hyre sone, in the west contre, and I trow that as tomorow ere ellys the next daye the Kyng Edwarde wyll depart from hense to hyre warde to dryve her owt ageyn.... As for Queen Margaret, I understand that she is removed from Windsor to Wallingford, nigh to Ewelme, my Lady of Suffolk's place in Oxfordshire.*

Also disappointing is Philip de Commines' *Memoires*. As Chamberlain at the court of Charles of Burgundy, de Commines met and observed several of the leading lights of both warring factions. While he was able to give a detailed account of Charles' support of Edward and to describe the circumstances surrounding Edward's departure for England, he had no first-hand knowledge of events following the landing at Ravenspur or of the Battle of Barnet itself.

Chapter Two

THE WARS OF THE ROSES

DISPUTES OVER SUCCESSION to a throne are usually attributable to the absence of a male heir. In the case of the Wars of the Roses, however, the difficulty lay in the fact that Edward III (1327–77) sired too many sons, five of whom survived to manhood. The eldest, Edward, the celebrated 'Black Prince', died in 1376, but his son, Richard, ruled England as Richard II from 1377 until his own ignominious death in 1399. Edward III's second surviving son, Lionel, Duke of Clarence, died in 1368. He fathered

King Henry V.

By 1453, England's once impressive spread of territorial possessions in France had shrunk to a single foothold – the port of Calais. It is thought that Henry VI's inability to retain his father's continental empire preyed upon his mind, hastening the onset of mental illness.

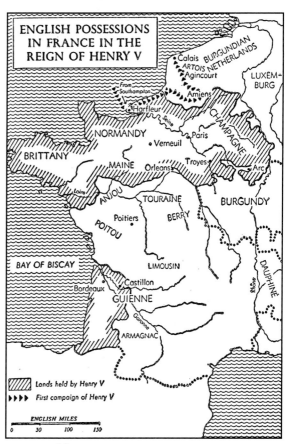

ENGLISH POSSESSIONS IN FRANCE IN THE REIGN OF HENRY V

Lands held by Henry V

First campaign of Henry V

ENGLISH MILES

19

The Houses of York and Lancaster

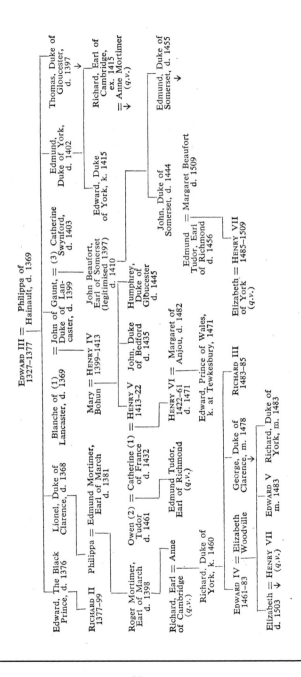

only a daughter, Philippa. Therefore, upon Richard II's death, the offspring of Edward III's third son, John of Gaunt, Duke of Lancaster, laid claim to the throne. The reigns of Henry IV (1399–1413) and Henry V (1413–22) followed.

With the accession of Henry VI in 1422, the problems really began. The line of Edward III's fourth son, Edmund, Duke of York, became linked through marriage with the line of Lionel, Duke of Clarence. This consolidated line became known as the House of York. A fifth son of Edward III, Thomas, Duke of Gloucester, had died without issue in 1397, thus leaving two rival family factions: the Houses of York and Lancaster.

At the time of his succession to the throne, the Lancastrian Henry VI was not yet one year old. Henry's infancy and subsequent insanity constituted the immediate cause of the Wars of the Roses, with representatives of the Houses of Lancaster and York competing with one another for control of the kingdom.

In the years leading up to the Wars of the Roses, the two main contenders for power were Richard, Duke of York, and Edmund Beaufort, 2nd Duke of Somerset, who aligned himself with Henry and his queen, Margaret of Anjou. In 1453 Henry suffered his first bout of insanity and Somerset took the blame for the nation's ultimate defeat in the Hundred Years' War with France. The Duke of York became Lord Protector. When Henry temporarily recovered his sanity, York was dismissed and Somerset returned to favour.

In 1455, York began the Wars of the Roses by openly challenging Henry and Margaret at the First Battle of St Albans. Somerset was killed and Henry captured, enabling York to become Lord Protector once more – only to be dismissed by Queen Margaret a year later. An uneasy peace prevailed until 1459, when open warfare broke out once more, this time resulting in Yorkist defeats at Blore Heath and Ludford Bridge. In July 1460, a Yorkist victory at the Battle of Northampton saw Henry captured again. Despite having a son (Prince Edward), Henry was forced to agree that the Duke of York would succeed him. York's future seemed to be assured, but at the end of the year a Lancastrian victory at Wakefield resulted in his death.

The Yorkist torch now passed to Richard's eldest son, Edward, Earl of March, who was supported in his endeavours by his cousin Richard Neville, Earl of Warwick. In 1461 Edward defeated the Lancastrians at Mortimer's Cross, a victory which was offset by Warwick's defeat at the Second Battle of St Albans. Notwithstanding their result at St Albans, Henry and Margaret withdrew to the North, enabling Edward to enter London and assume the crown as King Edward IV. In a 'final' pitched battle at Towton on 29 March 1461, the Lancastrians were overwhelmed. Henry, Margaret, Prince Edward and Henry Beaufort, 3rd Duke of Somerset, made for Scotland.

Edward's Act of Attainder comprised over 130 names, yet Lancastrian resistance continued for the next three years, which at least had the effect of preserving Yorkist unity. Margaret sought the help of the French king, Louis XI, but a punitive expedition, supported by the Scots, which landed at Bamborough in

Richard Neville Earl of Warwick called 'The Kingmaker' and his wife Anne Beauchamp from the Rous Roll. GEOFFREY WHEELER

Northumberland came to nought. Two relatively minor battles were fought between Somerset and Warwick's brother, Lord Montagu, at Hedgeley Moor and Hexham in 1464. Somerset came off worst in both encounters. Captured at Hexham, he was summarily executed.

Despite its success, by 1469 the House of York was divided. With Henry VI safely tucked away in the Tower of London and Margaret in exile, Edward IV had ruled for nine years, yet relations between himself and the Earl of Warwick had become strained to breaking point. The bone of contention was Edward's marriage to Elizabeth Woodville, which had been entered into without the approval of Warwick, who had a French marriage in mind for the king. To some extent this was merely a symptom of the real problem, which was Edward's desire to rule independently of 'the Kingmaker', without whose support he might never have seized the throne. Even so, the Woodvilles were very unpopular with the Yorkist 'old guard', at whose expense they profited handsomely in terms of preferment.

Believing that what he had done before he could do again, Warwick cast his net upon the waters and snared Edward's pliable brother, the Duke of Clarence. In July 1469, at Calais, Clarence married Warwick's eldest daughter, Isabella. Immediately afterwards, Warwick and Clarence issued a challenge to Edward, demanding redress for their grievances, linked with their own return and a planned resurrection in the North of England.

In response to rumours of discontent, Edward marched north, but was unable to venture beyond Nottingham owing to the widespread hostility he encountered en route. There, he awaited the Earl of Pembroke who was approaching from the west with reinforcements. The northern rebels, led by a shadowy figure known as 'Robin of Redesdale', were already on the move, and on 26 July they encountered – and defeated – Pembroke at Edgcote in Northamptonshire.

Edward was apprehended and taken to Middleham Castle, but Warwick discovered that he was unable to command the loyalty of hardcore Lancastrians and soon had to release him. Although Edward was able to re-establish his authority after a fashion, he remained shaken, perhaps fully appreciating for the first time the precarious nature of his hold on power.

Unfazed, Warwick and Clarence went on to exploit a private disagreement between a member of the king's household, Sir Thomas Burgh, and one of Warwick's relations, Lord Welles. When Edward intervened on Sir Thomas' behalf, Welles' son, Sir Robert,

Warwick escorts the captive Henry VI 'in an old blue gown' into London for his brief restoration as king. GEOFFREY WHEELER raised an armed force, intending to join up with Warwick, who had been given permission to raise an army in the king's name. The conjunction did not take place, and on 12 March 1470 Edward defeated Sir Robert near Stamford at the Battle of Losecoat Field, so called because the rebels discarded their livery – found to be Clarence's – as they ran. The game was up. Warwick and Clarence were denounced as potential traitors and fled the country.

Warwick now turned to his arch enemy, Margaret of Anjou. He proposed a marriage between his daughter Anne and Margaret's son Prince Edward. After Warwick had knelt before her and begged her forgiveness, Margaret agreed to join forces with him. With men and supplies readily donated by Louis XI, Warwick returned to England, landing on the south coast on 13 September.

Another ruse – Edward seems to have been particularly susceptible to ruses – drew the king off to the north. Challenged at Pontefract by Lord Montagu, he panicked, fleeing through Lincolnshire to King's Lynn from where, in company with the Duke of Gloucester and Lord Hastings, he sailed for the Low Countries, leaving his wife and mother-in-law to seek the sanctuary of Westminster Abbey.

On 6 October 1470 Henry VI was restored and Lancastrians were appointed/reappointed to key positions in government. Edward IV

Edward IV of the House of York was dethroned and declared a traitor. GEOFFREY WHEELER

Henry VI of the House of Lancaster was returned to the throne.

Richard, Duke of Gloucester

Richard, Duke of Gloucester, began life at Fotheringhay in Northamptonshire on 2 October 1452, one of thirteen children born to Richard and Cecily, Duke and Duchess of York. While the Duke's eldest surviving sons, Edward and Edmund, shared their father's vicissitudes during the early years of the Wars of the Roses, the younger pair, George and Richard, were consigned to the care of their mother. In 1459, for reasons of safety, the family was moved to Ludlow Castle. As strange as it may seem, this was the first occasion on which Richard and Edward met.

The meeting was short, for when Ludlow was threatened by a Lancastrian army the Duke of York fled, together with Edward, Edmund and the Earl of Warwick. Cecily fell into Lancastrian hands and was placed in the custody of her elder sister, the staunchly Lancastrian Duchess of Buckingham. According to one account, at Edward's behest the Archbishop of Canterbury cared for George and Richard.

The Duke of York's return and his bid for the crown merely increased the ever-present danger surrounding his children. When the Duke and his son, Edmund, were killed at Wakefield in December 1460, Cecily, with the aid of the Earl of Warwick, arranged for George and Richard to be sent to Burgundy to ensure their safety.

They remained abroad until 1461, by which time the House of York was in the ascendant once more, Edward having become King Edward IV by virtue of the Yorkist victory at Towton. Richard and George returned home to participate in their brother's coronation. Both were made Knights of the Garter and George was created Duke of Clarence, while Richard took his father's title of Duke of Gloucester. For some time afterwards they lived in the medieval splendour of Greenwich Palace until, perhaps, 1465, when according to one contemporary account Edward 'entered them into the practice of arms'.

For the next few years Richard was engaged in military

training, probably at Middleham Castle, under the tutelage of the Earl of Warwick. Little is known about these formative years, but he did forge lasting friendships with two other boys, Robert Percy and Francis Lovell. It is also certain that he learned much which would prove invaluable in helping to bring about Warwick's defeat at Barnet.

In 1465 the growing estrangement between Edward and Warwick led to Richard's departure from Middleham. He spent much of the next five years at court, where life was dominated by the Woodvilles. Unlike George, who became Warwick's willing collaborator, Richard remained loyal to Edward. When Warwick later detained Edward in 1469, Richard escaped arrest. He may have avoided Warwick's clutches, or pehaps Warwick thought that he had established a sufficiently strong bond with his erstwhile student to negate any threat he might conceivably pose.

Richard's loyalty was amply rewarded when Edward regained his freedom. He was appointed Constable of England and Chief Justice of North Wales. In the latter capacity he put down a Welsh rebellion and was subsequently made Chief Justice of South Wales. Clearly, Edward was placing more and more trust in his brother, and when he was himself driven into temporary exile in 1470 he was accompanied by Richard – truly a man for all seasons.

Warwick landing at Calais. GEOFFREY WHEELER

now assumed the role of traitor, while Warwick and Clarence were confirmed as Lieutenants of the Realm. The credulity of contemporary chroniclers, who marvelled at the pace of change, would have been stretched to the limits had they known that, within six months, the wheel would turn full circle yet again.

Chapter Three

THE BATTLE OF BARNET: PRELUDE

ON 6 OCTOBER 1470, Richard Neville, Earl of Warwick, George, Duke of Clarence, George Neville, Archbishop of York, John Talbot, Earl of Shrewsbury, and Thomas, Lord Stanley, entered London in triumph. A dishevelled King Henry was liberated from the Tower and, clad in a blue velvet gown, was deposited in the Bishop of London's palace, where Warwick also established himself.

Warwick lost no time in getting a grip on the country. The Archbishop of York resumed charge of the Great Seal, John Hales, Bishop of Lichfield, received the Privy Seal, and Sir John Langstrother was appointed Lord High Treasurer. Clarence was reappointed Lieutenant of Ireland, a post he retrieved from the Earl of Worcester, who furnished the government with its only execution. Amid a general amnesty, the leading Yorkists who had not accompanied Edward into exile – notably the Earl of Essex and the Duke of Norfolk – were taken on board, but there was no place in the new administration for some of Warwick's own staunchest supporters, such as the Earls of Oxford and Shrewsbury, and Lord Stanley.

Complex at the best of times, the global situation became positively labyrinthine. The Lancastrian king, Henry VI was now – nominally – the reigning monarch. The true ruler, as 'Lieutenant of England,' was the Yorkist rebel Earl of Warwick. In exile, under the protection of his brother-in-law, the Duke of Burgundy, was the Yorkist king, Edward IV. Also still in exile, under the protection of Louis XI of France, was the Lancastrian Queen Margaret of Anjou.

Edward wanted the Duke of Burgundy to help him regain power, but the Duke was prepared to accept any English monarch in the interests of maintaining the peace. Henry remained a pawn in the game, for Margaret looked to Louis for help in her own return to England and assumption of her position as the power behind the throne. Louis wanted to use Warwick as an ally to make war on Burgundy. Warwick had to please nearly everybody.

At least Edward had only to please Charles. Patience was not the

Yorkist king's forte, but he was entirely dependent upon his brother-in-law, and although Charles settled a generous allowance upon him he showed little inclination to do much more. Apart from his desire to keep the peace his personal preference had always been for the House of Lancaster. He was quick to drop the hint that any king acceptable to the English would also be acceptable to him, so Edward was kept at arm's length for three months.

Despite Charles' best angling, however, Warwick did not take the bait. Louis XI, keen to gain the upper hand against Burgundy, kept Warwick dangling on his own hook. On 14 October, Louis proclaimed a treaty of alliance with the House of Lancaster, with free trade for all who recognized Henry as king. In November a three days' thanksgiving was held in Paris for Henry's restoration, while Margaret and the Prince and Princess of Wales were brought to Paris in state. Envoys were sent to London to cajole Warwick, and encourage hostility towards Burgundy. In return for his participation in hostilities, Warwick was promised Holland and Zealand. On 28 November an alliance against Burgundy was signed in Paris, the Prince of Wales signing on behalf of his father. On 3 December, Louis announced his rejection of the Treaty of Péronne (signed between France and Burgundy in 1468), and a week later he seized St Quentin, following up with attacks on Roye, Montdidier and Amiens.

Charles responded by finally sending for Edward. Between 2 and 7 January 1471, the pair were locked in negotiations, resulting in the Duke's promise to grant Edward the sum of 50,000 florins and such ships as were necessary to mount an assault on England. Charles was taking a terrible risk, but, caught between the proverbial rock and a hard place, he had little choice but to throw in his lot with the House of York.

When it became known that Warwick had concluded an alliance with France, his fragile popularity suffered. As the ex-Yorkist power behind the Lancastrian throne, he was viewed with suspicion. The presence of Queen Margaret would have helped to regularize his position, but she stayed on in France, preferring to bide her time rather than stake everything on supporting what seemed to many to be a shaky and, indeed, illegitimate administration. Nevertheless, Warwick put his faith in her imminent arrival. In February he even went down to Dover to meet her, but nearly two months would elapse before she set foot in England.

Clarence constituted another problem. Despite nominally sharing the 'lieutenancy' of England with Warwick, he had no real voice in the new administration and always hankered after the crown. His loyalties remained uncertain, and Warwick must have been aware of efforts that Clarence's mother and sisters were making to coax him back into the Yorkist fold. In fact Warwick's brain must have been spinning. With a fluid balance of power and consequent shifting loyalties, whose favour did he need to court, and who could he afford to ignore?

Fortunately, Warwick's stature and reputation were sufficient in themselves to secure obedience. He knew that any challenge to his authority would come, via the sea, from Edward. Retaining the key position of High Admiral, therefore, he appointed the Earl of Oxford and Lord Scrope to guard the east coast, while Lord Montagu and Jasper Tudor kept watch in the north and west respectively.

Meanwhile, across the North Sea, the generous, albeit tardy and expedient, support of the Duke of Burgundy enabled Edward to cobble together an invasion fleet. On 2 March 1471 Edward boarded his flagship at Flushing. Although the wind was against him he kept his men on board for nine days, until the 11th, when the wind changed, enabling him finally to set sail accompanied by, among others, the Duke of Gloucester, Earl Rivers and the Lords Hastings and Saye. Their army of liberation comprised 1,200 men, a quarter of whom were Dutch mercenaries.

The fleet sailed directly for the Norfolk coast and on 12 March anchored off Cromer. A small party led by Sir Robert Chamberlain and Sir Gilbert Debenham, sent ashore to canvass support, found little to cheer them, the Earl of Oxford having a tight grip on the eastern counties, while potential supporters such as the Duke of Norfolk had been called to London, where Warwick could keep them under scrutiny. Having received this dis-couraging report, Edward decided to sail on northwards – and straight into a storm. For two days the expedition was at the mercy of tempestuous seas, but on Thursday 14 March Edward's own ship docked at Ravenspur, at the mouth of the River Humber.

In company with many settlements along this brittle stretch of coastline, Ravenspur has long since been swept away into the ocean. So completely has it vanished that its exact location remains a mystery. However, Edward was by no means creeping into the country by the back door, for medieval Ravenspur was acknowledged as one of the wealthiest and most flourishing ports in the kingdom, hosting an annual fair of thirty days, holding two markets a week and returning two Members of Parliament. And,

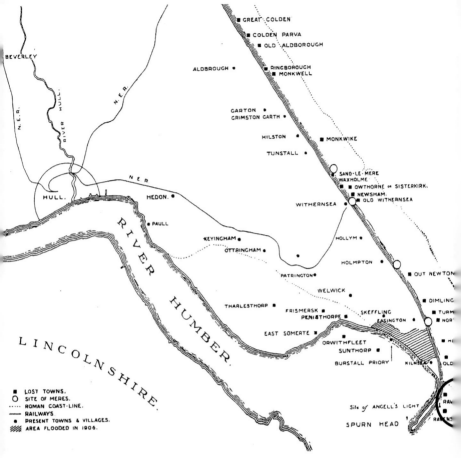

Possible location, off Spurn Head, of Ravenspur (or 'Ravenspurn'), one of the many medieval settlements which have been washed away into the North Sea.

with a neat touch of irony, it was also the place where, in 1399, Henry of Bolingbroke had landed to dethrone Richard II.

The storm had caused the fleet to become dispersed, and the other ships landed wherever they could – the Duke of Gloucester came ashore four miles away, while Earl Rivers made land some fourteen miles distant, at Paul. Thus Edward's first night back on English soil was fraught with danger as, in relative isolation, he lay camped two miles inland.

During the course of the following day (15 March) everyone managed to find their way to Edward's campsite, and a council of war was held. Ideally, Edward wanted to press on to London. The speediest route would take him through Lincolnshire, which meant crossing the Humber. He was loath to do this, as to take to the water again might be interpreted as a retreat, in addition to which he would be marching through potentially unfriendly territory. The Yorkshiremen who had gathered to meet him were less than co-operative, but they seemed to be responsive to the idea that he wished primarily to claim his rightful inheritance as Duke of York, the title held by his father. So, it was agreed that he should march to York, a decision which at least had the effect of staving off an immediate confrontation. Hull having closed its gates against him, Edward struck out for York via Beverley, while armed detachments watched his movements warily.

Three miles south of the city he was met by the Recorder of York, Thomas Conyers, who tried to discourage him from going any further, advising him that the gates were closed against him. If by any chance he did effect an entry, said Conyers, he would be 'lost and undone'. Yet, trusting to luck, Edward pressed on. Before he reached the city itself he was accosted by two additional envoys, Robert Clifford and Richard Burgh who were more conciliatory, assuring him that in his capacity of claimant for the Duchy of York

This old engraving of Fotheringhay depicts St Mary's Church with the castle mound to its rear. Once a grand and imposing structure that dominated the landscape, Fotheringhay Castle was permitted to fall into disrepair and was demolished soon after 1635, the internal and external fabric being utilised in the construction of many local buildings. Owned from 1415 by Richard, Duke of York, the castle was the birthplace of the Duke of Gloucester.

he would be allowed to enter. Conyers again tried to dissuade him, but when he reached Walmgate Bar Clifford and Burgh led him within, accompanied by fifteen or sixteen of his companions. He managed to convince the leading citizens of his supposedly limited intentions, and went so far as to call for cheers for King Henry and Prince Edward. His whole force was then admitted and entertained for the night. The next morning (19 March) they set out for Tadcaster, a town associated with the Earl of Northumberland.

It may be wondered why Warwick had done nothing to check his old protégé's progress. The failure to nip the invasion in the bud was largely due to the rivalry of the two Earls of Northumberland. Henry Percy, the current earl, was by rights a Lancastrian, but he owed his promotion to Edward. Unable to carry his followers into the Yorkist camp, he kept them at a distance, leaving the ex-earl, John Neville, Lord Montagu, afraid to act alone in a district where Warwick and Henry together should have been all-powerful.

Another day on the road brought Edward to Sandal Castle and the scene of the Battle of Wakefield, where his father had met his death. Contrary to his expectations, recruitment remained poor. Montagu was at Pontefract Castle but, like the armed bands which had hovered menacingly in the shadows since the expedition's landing, he balked at the prospect of sallying forth to tackle Edward's compact but determined force. Thankful that his progress was not impeded, Edward continued on to Doncaster and, from there, to Nottingham, where on 25 March he was joined by Sir William Parre and Sir James Harrington, 'with two good bands of men'.

At Nottingham he also learned that twenty miles to the north-east, at Newark, the Duke of Exeter, the Earl of Oxford and Viscount Beaumont had amassed an opposition force of 4,000 men gleaned from the counties of Essex, Norfolk, Suffolk, Cambridgeshire, Huntingdonshire and Lincolnshire. Edward advanced to face them, but when he was still three miles from the town he learned that they had fled during the previous night, having panicked at the approach of his scouts, whom they mistook for his entire army.

Fortune favours the bold, and it was certainly favouring Edward. His dispersed forces could have been annihilated on landing; he might have been mauled by any one of a number of armed bodies of men en route to York; his progress could have been checked at Pontefract by Montagu; and, without doubt, he should have been challenged at Newark. Instead, he was able to march on to Leicester,

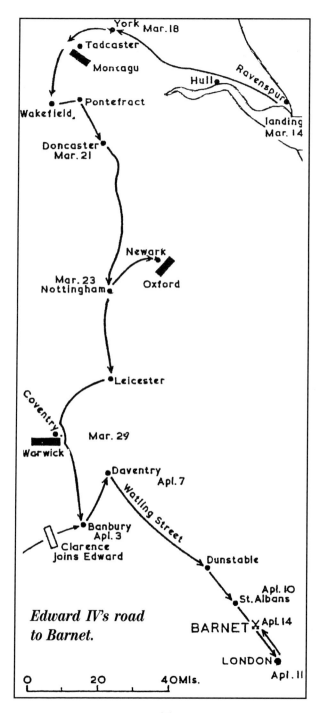

York Mar. 18
Tadcaster
Montagu
Ravenspur
Hull
landing Mar. 14
Wakefield
Pontefract
Doncaster
Mar. 21
Newark
Mar. 23
Nottingham
Oxford
Leicester
Coventry
Mar. 29
Warwick
Daventry
Apl. 7
Watling Street
Banbury
Apl. 3
Clarence
joins Edward
Dunstable
Apl. 10
St. Albans
*Edward IV's road
to Barnet.*
BARNET ╳ Apl. 14
LONDON
Apl. 11

0   20   40 Mls.

where Warwick awaited him.

Even though he led an army of around 6,000 men, Warwick lost his nerve, and instead of confronting Edward he retreated to Coventry and, on 27 March, took refuge within its walls. This was the turning point of the campaign, Warwick's negativity resulting in many of those who wavered declaring for Edward. It was certainly the signal for Edward to set out his stall. On 29 March he appeared under the walls of Coventry and challenged Warwick to come out, but the earl, his support waning, refused. Edward then advanced to Warwick Castle and, throwing caution to the wind, proclaimed himself king.

Both Edward and Warwick were aware that Clarence was approaching with men raised in Henry's name, but Edward appeared to be confident that his brother, bound by filial duty, would rejoin him. It is unclear whether Warwick knew of Clarence's intentions, but having himself benefited by his duplicity, he must have had his suspicions. Remaining ensconced in Coventry, Warwick did make an effort to draw Edward into negotiations. Edward responded by offering quarter to Warwick and his troops upon their surrender.

While the earl played for time, Clarence approached. Edward went forth to meet him, an encounter which took place three miles outside Warwick on the road to Banbury. Also well aware that, brother or not, Clarence could not be trusted, Edward may have been expecting trouble, but he need not have worried. The two men, each accompanied by a small retinue, met in sight of their armies and made their peace. Edward must have noted that the coats of Clarence's troops displayed the Lancastrian Collar with the Yorkshire Rose over it – such was the haste with which Clarence, always with an eye for the main chance, had changed his colours.

Although he had declared for his brother, Clarence proceeded to assume the role of honest broker, acting as a go-between for Edward and Warwick, forwarding messages to and fro. Whatever Edward's sentiments towards Warwick may have been, however, the earl knew that he had burned his bridges. He had driven Edward into exile, entered into an alliance with Edward's sworn enemies and, should he yield, it was unlikely that he could look forward to anything better than incarceration in the Tower.

Disappointed though Warwick may have been at Clarence's defection, he had been reinforced by Montagu and the Earl of Oxford. Even so, he still refused to give battle, perhaps hoping that Queen Margaret would yet make an appearance. Unwilling to waste any more time, Edward resolved to make for London, to oust Henry from the seat of government. After Warwick had refused one final offer to come out and fight, Edward resumed his southward march, posting a strong rearguard as a deterrent against any active pursuit. On Palm Sunday he paused at Daventry. From there, he proceeded to Northampton, where he was 'well received', and Dunstable, reaching St Albans on 10 April, where he rested again.

The consternation and confusion in London to which his approach gave rise may well be imagined. The Archbishop of York convened an emergency meeting of leading Lancastrians at St Paul's. They decided to show their muscle by driving a military parade, featuring the Lancastrian king, through the streets, and Henry was taken on a circuitous tour from the Bishop's Palace, where he lodged, through Cheapside to Walbrook and back to St Paul's. This exercise in punitive pageantry backfired, for the sight of the feeble-minded monarch, who probably had no idea of what was happening, did little to foster public confidence in his ability to counter any assault on the capital.

In addition many of the leading Lancastrian lights were out of town. As the Earl of Warwick had hoped, Queen Margaret, in company with, among others, the Prince of Wales, the Countess of Warwick and Lord Wenlock, was expected to land in the West Country. Accordingly, the Duke of Somerset, the Marquis of Dorset and the Earl of Devon had journeyed down there in order to raise an

The Tower of London in late medieval times.

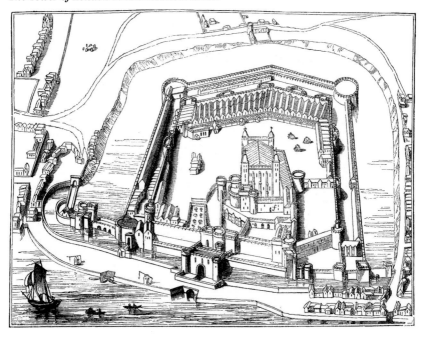

army to welcome and reinforce her expedition. But Margaret had tarried too long, for she remained in France, at the mercy of unfavourable winds.

Taking into consideration the rumoured strength of Edward's army, the capital's leading dignitaries decided to admit him and sent word to that effect. Bowing to the inevitable, the Archbishop of York jumped ship and sent his own messages to Edward, pledging his undying loyalty. During the night, the Tower and city gates were seized on Edward's behalf, and the next day, 11 April, at noon, Edward rode into London in triumph. He made straight for St Paul's and took the hapless Henry into custody. He next visited Westminster Abbey, where he 'made his devout prayers', giving thanks to God and the Saints Peter and Edward. His queen, Elizabeth, had continued to live in Westminster sanctuary – a gloomy building occupying a space at the end of St Margaret's churchyard – where she had given birth to a son, Prince Edward, destined for a grisly end at the hands of Uncle Richard. But this was for the future. For the present, king and queen were reunited. Following a speedy coronation, they stayed with Edward's mother, the Duchess of York, hearing divine service that night and the next morning, Good Friday.

A depiction of the Kingmaker roustin[g] his forces prior to the Battle of Barne[t]. Having played the turncoat from Yor[k] to Lancaster he faced the prospect [of] meeting his former protégé, Edward I[V,] on the field of battle.

BASED ON A TABLEAU AT WARWICK CASTLE

There was still much to be done, for Warwick had been quick to vacate Coventry once Edward had departed. It was unlikely that he would be able to overtake him, but he hoped that London would refuse to open its gates. Even if worse came to worst and Edward did gain admission, Warwick felt sure that Edward would observe Easter, thereby handing him the opportunity to launch a surprise attack. He sent riders to London, begging the Archbishop of York

Marching Orders

In *Battles and Battlefields in England*, C.R.B. Barrett observes that 'of two armies *caeteris paribus* the one which possesses the greatest mobility possesses considerable superiority over the other' – and the campaign trails relating to battles fought on British soil do contain some examples of remarkable marches. King Harold's 200-mile trek from London to York in 1066 and Prince Rupert's monumental march of 1644, much of it through hostile territory, to raise the siege of York are two cases in point.

In times of civil war, speed of movement can be of paramount importance. During the southern campaigns of the English Civil War, Charles I was never able to conjure up sufficient speed to beat the enemy to London, while Edward IV's speedy progress from Coventry to London was crucial to his ultimate success.

Mobility was governed partly by the necessity of taking a route which provided an army with opportunities to forage for food, and still more by the condition of the roads. In the fifteenth century, beyond a few improvements made during the reign of Edward I, Roman roads still formed the nucleus of the communications system and, as Barrett points out, it is no coincidence that many significant battles fought on English soil have been fought in close proximity to Roman roads. In the Wars of the Roses alone, both battles of St Albans, as well as Northampton, Towton, Empingham, Barnet and Stoke Field, spring readily to mind.

In terms of the Barnet campaign, tracing Edward IV's immediate route from Ravenspur is fairly straightforward. We do not know the location of Ravenspur, beyond the fact that it was not too far from Spurn Head. However, Edward probably picked up a track following the course of a Roman road in the vicinity of Patrington, which he would have followed via Wawne Ferry to Beverley. After his emissaries had been turned away from Hull, he continued on directly to York. From York, he struck out for Tadcaster and from there to Sandal Castle, near Wakefield. He reached Doncaster on 21 March. Again, this portion of the march was accomplished along tried and trusted portions of Ermine Street.

Intelligence regarding the route of the march through the

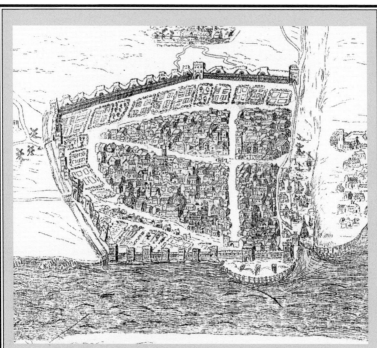

Hull, Lancastrian in sympathy, closed its gates against Edward IV. In a later civil war, admission would be refused to another monarch: Charles I.

Midlands – Nottingham, Leicester, Warwick and Coventry – is more sketchy. On the final leg from Banbury, however, he headed north to Daventry via Chipping Warden, along a track which followed the course of the present-day A361. From Daventry he marched to Northampton, and from there along Watling Street to London, via Dunstable and St Albans.

Edward's progress from Ravenspur to London must rank as one of the greatest marches in English military history. From an inauspicious landing, and accompanied by relatively few followers, he made his way through potentially hostile country, running a very real risk of attack at any moment. A blend of Yorkist guile, bluff and raw courage opened the road to the finishing post and a well deserved triumph.

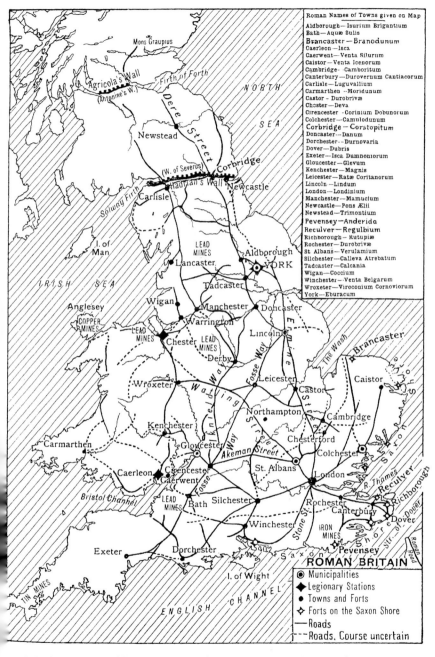

Roman Names of Towns given on Map

Aldborough — Isurium Brigantium
Bath — Aquæ Sulis
Brancaster — Branodunum
Caerleon — Isca
Caerwent — Venta Silurum
Caistor — Venta Icenorum
Cambridge — Camboritum
Canterbury — Durovernum Cantiacorum
Carlisle — Luguvallium
Carmarthen — Moridunum
Castor — Durobrivæ
Chester — Deva
Cirencester — Corinium Dobunorum
Colchester — Camulodunum
Corbridge — Corstopitum
Doncaster — Danum
Dorchester — Durnovaria
Dover — Dubris
Exeter — Isca Dumnoniorum
Gloucester — Glevum
Kenchester — Magnis
Leicester — Ratæ Coritanorum
Lincoln — Lindum
London — Londinium
Manchester — Mamucium
Newcastle — Pons Ælii
Newstead — Trimontium
Pevensey — Anderida
Reculver — Regulbium
Richborough — Rutupiæ
Rochester — Durobrivæ
St Albans — Verulamium
Silchester — Calleva Atrebatum
Tadcaster — Calcania
Wigan — Coccium
Winchester — Venta Belgarum
Wroxeter — Viroconium Cornoviorum
York — Eburacum

ROMAN BRITAIN

◉ Municipalities
◆ Legionary Stations
● Towns and Forts
✦ Forts on the Saxon Shore
— Roads
--- Roads, Course uncertain

Britain's network of Roman roads – still very much depended upon for long-distance travel in the Middle Ages.

41

Seal of Richard Neville, Earl of Warwick, as Lord Glamorgan and Morgannwg.
GEOFFREY WHEELER

The obverse shows him mounted on a horse bearing the arms of Montacote and Mortermer on the shoulder. The reverse shows the many quarterings supported by his bear badge and surmounted by two helms.
GEOFFREY WHEELER

and the Mayor and Aldermen to hold out until he arrived.

There was every reason for hope. After all, in addition to Warwick's own army Queen Margaret was still expected to land at any moment, and Lord Fauconberg was known to be recruiting in Kent. On paper, at least, there could soon be three Lancastrian armies ready to converge on London. Yet in his heart Warwick, old campaigner that he was, must have known the game was up. His best chance for defeating Edward had passed him by. As he advanced towards London, he heard that Edward had been received and that the Archbishop of York, his own brother, had abandoned him.

Chapter Four

THE BATTLE OF BARNET

DESPITE HIS WELCOME by the citizens of London, Edward was far from home and dry. With Warwick advancing on the capital, the final test was yet to come. On the afternoon of 13 April – Easter Saturday – Edward marched out of London with 'a great armye', well prepared to meet Warwick's challenge. The men with whom he had landed were weary enough, but there were new recruits to swell his ranks, together with fresh supplies and equipment. Henry VI was taken along as a hostage.

A march of ten miles brought the Yorkists to Barnet. According to the Arrivall, Edward's scouts encountered a party of Warwick's men and put them to flight, driving them out of the village 'more some what than an halfe myle', until, 'undre an hedge-sydc', they came upon Warwick's main force, variously described as 'redy assembled' and 'in array'.

From St Albans, Warwick, too, had marched ten miles, along rough tracks via Colney, South Mimms, The Wash, Dancers Hill and Kitts End. His final position was well chosen, his army occupying Gladmore Heath (the present-day Hadley Green), an expanse of rising ground which falls away to the south, in what was the direction of Edward's approach. It has been suggested that Warwick would have been better advised to occupy Barnet in force, but his experience at the First Battle of St Albans probably made him wary of the uncertainties of urban warfare. He would also have found it difficult to maintain discipline if his men were let loose in the town.

First in the field, Warwick had plenty of time to consider his options and, by selecting his ground as he did, he was able to

Monken Hadley, as depicted on the 1822 Ordnance Survey map.

present an extended front on high ground from beyond a moated manor house, 'Old Fold', to a point above St Mary's Church. The ground to his rear fell away gently to the west and rather more sharply to the east. The land which lay before him was more uneven, dipping between the church and the spot he chose for his left wing. This depression added to the strength of his position, for it would have to be negotiated by an attacking force.

By the time Edward came up with his army night had fallen. His men must have been hoping to take their rest in the town but, for the same reasons as Warwick, he did not linger and advanced beyond it to camp on its northern outskirts, disposing his men 'in good arraye' and issuing an order that, as far as possible, silence must be maintained.

What is reasonably certain is that the two armies were no more than 500yds (457m) apart. With thousands of men in such close proximity, complete silence could not be maintained. Conditions were so cramped that 'what for the neighying of horses and talkynge of menne, none of both the hostes could that night take any rest of quietnes'. Worst of all, perhaps, for the Yorkists, no campfires were allowed. Throughout the night, Warwick's artillery – in which he is said to have been the stronger – fired into the darkness in the general direction of the Yorkist camp, though most of the cannon balls overshot their mark as it was not imagined that the enemy could be so near. Thus the hours wore on, an eerie silence finally settling over the scene as each man, focusing on the battle to come, retreated into his private world of uncertainty and fear.

Dawn brought with it the first of a series of surprises – all of which were destined to work in the Yorkists' favour – as the darkness was replaced not by daylight, but by 'a greate myste', so that each army could discern the other only indistinctly. Nevertheless, the opposing leaders marshalled their forces. The Earl of Oxford led the Lancastrian right, while the Duke of Exeter commanded the left, with Lord Montagu in the centre. Cavalry was placed on each wing. Warwick's own position is uncertain, but it is likely that, initially at least, he remained in the rear, perhaps with a reserve. (It has been suggested that Edmund Beaufort, the fourth Duke of Somerset, commanded the Lancastrian centre, but it is probable that he was on the south coast, awaiting the arrival of Margaret of Anjou. It seems very unlikely that he could have escaped, unscathed, from Barnet.)

It is important to note here that the Lancastrian leadership was a

Hadley Green, marking the Yorkist centre ground.

strange alliance. Oxford and Exeter were hereditary Lancastrians, but Warwick's change of colours had been born of resentment, while Montagu, a personal friend of Edward, had been curiously reticent to challenge him during his march from York. Mistrust figured prominently in the Wars of the Roses, and the fear of betrayal was never far from the minds of the principal players.

Edward also massed his forces in three divisions. Citing *The Great Chronicle of London*, local historian Fiona Jones places Gloucester on the left wing and Hastings on the right. This may have been the case, but it is more likely that Gloucester would have been given pride of place on the right wing, with Hastings commanding the left, while Edward remained in the centre where the captive Henry VI may have been placed. Clarence was at Edward's side, where he, too, could be closely observed.

It is said that owing to the poor visibility Edward was deceived as to Warwick's deployment and that the right wing of his army, under Gloucester, strayed too far to the east, thereby overlapping

Edward IV with his artillery, cannon and bombards, of the type used at Barnet.

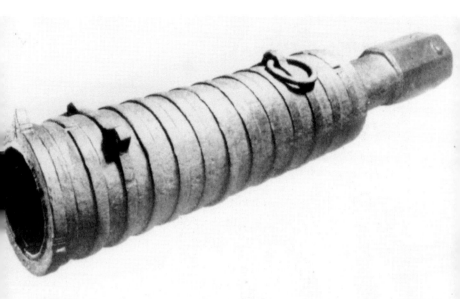

15th Century Iron Hooped 'bombard' or cannon. GEOFFREY WHEELER

Warwick's left wing. However, one would have thought that Edward's scouts, as a result of their earlier brush with the enemy, would have been able to provide reasonably accurate intelligence regarding Warwick's dispositions. If this were so, then Edward's own deployment may have been selected by design rather than by accident. Had the Yorkist army been drawn up in three 'battles' directly opposite the Lancastrians, then Hastings on the Yorkist left wing would have been placed at a disadvantage on much lower ground. Edward may well have had more confidence in Gloucester's ability to fight from a relatively unfavourable position, and so it was he who found himself having to negotiate difficult terrain.

As with most Roses encounters, it is difficult to assess, with any degree of accuracy, the numbers of participants. Invariably, contemporary and near-contemporary estimates were inflated as it was always in the winner's interest to maximize a victory by wildly exaggerating the strength of the opposition. Thus it was afterwards claimed that Warwick's host had been between 20,000 and 30,000 strong. However, as Burne has pointed out in The Battlefields of England, a little fieldwork suggests that the extent of the ridge along which the Lancastrians were massed would be 'a convenient length' for an army of around 15,000 men.

Just as the Yorkists were anxious to overestimate Warwick's

numbers, so they were inclined to underestimate their own. Oddly enough, modern estimates of the strength of Edward's army often tend to support contemporary partisan claims. The figure is put at between 8,000 and 9,000 men. However, it may be that the Yorkists actually outnumbered the Lancastrians. For example, a reliable source, Philippe de Comines, states that Clarence took over to

The Battle of Barnet (1). In the first phase of the battle, Oxford's outflanking manoeuvre on the Lancastrian right was to some extent counterbalanced by Gloucester's success on the opposite wing. This sketch map shows the Yorkist and Lancastrian deployment on a modern plan of the area. Both sides probably had reserves to the rear of their respective positions – the Lancastrian reserve being commanded by Warwick.

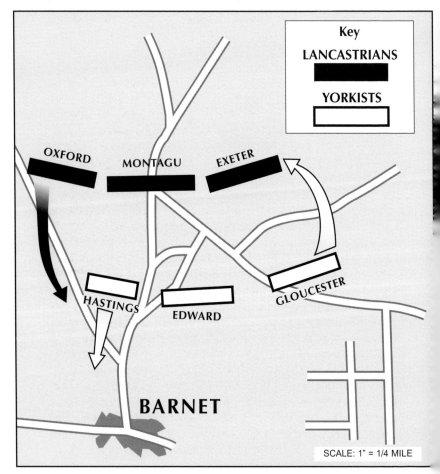

Edward a body of no less than 15,000 men. Even if this is disregarded, it is certain that up to the last moment, new recruits were flocking to Edward's banner. While any figure must remain in essence supposition, it may be fair to suggest that the two armies were quite evenly matched.

Contemporary chroniclers claim that Warwick encouraged his men with the assurance that they were fighting in the cause of a gentle and rightful sovereign against a tyrant who had invaded the realm, 'a cruell man and a tocious usurper', so that God must needs be their shield and defence. Edward, on the other hand, denounced his adversaries as traitors to the realm and spoilers of the poor commonality. It was good policy on his part to represent himself as the promoter of popular interests.

It is generally accepted that the battle began at about 5.00 am. Archers on either side first discharged their arrows, with the support, perhaps, of a limited artillery barrage. Before long, however, both sides 'joyned and came to hand-strokes'. The fight appears to have resolved into a succession of engagements over different parts of the field, not directed according to any fixed plan – an eventuality easily understood if the murkiness of the weather is taken into consideration. For a time the issue hung in the balance, and there was a period during the struggle when it must have seemed more than probable that victory would crown the efforts of the Lancastrians.

On the Yorkist right, things went well for Edward. Despite having to negotiate the depression between himself and Exeter, Gloucester made the most of the advantage afforded by the overlapping line. It was the first battle in which the eighteen-year-old had been engaged, but he acquitted himself well and 'entred so farre and boldly into the ennemies' army, that two of his esquires, Thomas Parr and John Milewater, being nearest to him, were slain; yet by his own valour he quit himselfe, and put most part of the enemies to flight'. In the process, Gloucester himself was slightly wounded.

To the Yorkist left it was a different story. As Gloucester had outflanked Exeter, so Montagu and Oxford outflanked Hastings, having 'a gretar distres upon the Kyngs party'. Hastings' men were routed and driven back in confusion into and beyond Barnet. So complete was the success of the manoeuvre that a number of the Yorkist fugitives carried on to London, spreading the news that 'the Kynge was distresyd and his fielde lost'. Fortunately for Edward, the mist concealed the plight of his left wing from the rest of the army.

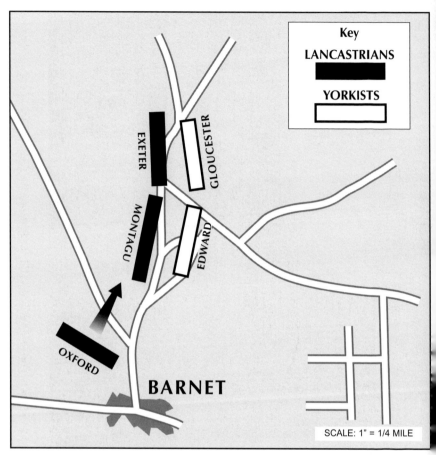

The Battle of Barnet (2). The second phase of the battle pivoted on the confusion arising from Oxford's return to a much changed field of action. Mistaken for Yorkists, his men were fired upon by their comrades.

The *Arrivall* ascribes Edward's final victory to his own commitment, as he 'mannly, vigorowsly, and valliantly' attacked the Lancastrian line at its strongest point, and 'with great violence, bett and bare down afore hym all that stode in hys way'. While Edward's personal courage is not in doubt, he owed his success to an incident of which the *Arrivall* makes no mention.

With Hastings' men running for their lives, Oxford's victorious soldiers had broken ranks. Preferring plunder to pursuit, they dispersed with a view to ransacking Barnet. By the time they had been rallied, the scenario on Gladmore Heath had changed. The

Broughton Church, Oxfordshire. Effigy of the Second Lord Saye, killed at the Battle of Barnet 1471. He wears the Yorkist collar of suns and roses.

GEOFFREY WHEELER

flanks of both armies had been turned, and the fighting had shifted on its axis from north-south to east-west. Thus the Lancastrian centre, and in particular the archers, now occupied the position vacated by Hastings.

The leading participants in the Wars of the Roses adopted a particular badge or device to identify their own retainers, this badge being embroidered upon their coats. Lord Oxford's device was a five-pointed star, which was very similar to that adopted by Edward IV, a sun with five rays – 'this sun of York', as Gloucester states in *Richard III*. The persistent fog was still 'so thycke, that a manne myghte not profytely juge one thynge from anothere'. Accordingly the Lancastrian archers, dimly aware of what appeared to be Edward's insignia adorning the tunics of the men now bearing down on them, loosed a volley of arrows into their ranks. Too late came the realization that this was not the enemy, but their own comrades. The spectre of treachery, which lingered over many a Roses' battlefield, now raised its head, and with cries of 'Treasoune! Treasoune!' Oxford's men turned upon their heels and fled the field – this time not to return.

Now was the time for Edward to introduce his reserves – fresh and vigorous soldiers ready to fight to the death for their king. Warwick, on the other hand, was compelled to call on men already exhausted, and the call went unanswered. The day was visibly lost. By 10.00 am, or noon at the latest, victory rested with the Yorkists

Uneven ground on Hadley Common, over which the Yorkist right wing commanded by the Duke of Gloucester was compelled to advance.

Effigy of Sir Henry Vernon. He refused to assist Warwick at Barnet after receiving his letter for help and similarly failed to aid Richard III's cause at Bosworth in 1485. GEOFFREY WHEELER

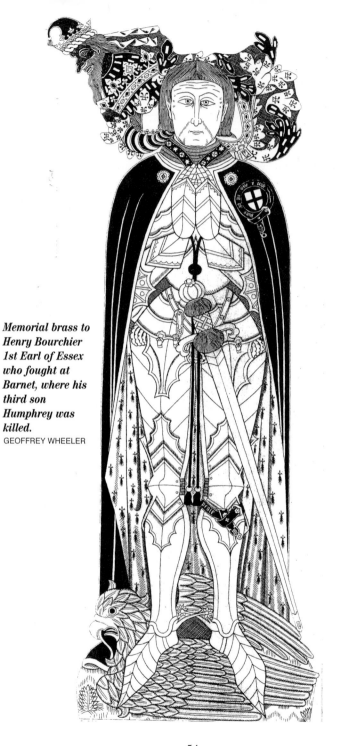

Memorial brass to Henry Bourchier 1st Earl of Essex who fought at Barnet, where his third son Humphrey was killed.

GEOFFREY WHEELER

and Warwick and Montagu lay dead upon the field.

How did Warwick die? Warkworth claims that Warwick 'lept one horse-backe and flede to a wode by the felde of Barnett, where was no waye forthe.' Seeing him, a Yorkist soldier 'came uppone hym and kylled hym, and dispolede hyme naked.' (Paul Murray Kendall draws a similar woeful picture, describing the 'gasping fight for breath' of 'a middle-aged man stumbling across a field'.) It is just possible that Edward tried to save him. All pretence of friendship and hopes of reconciliation had long-since evaporated, but Edward may have wished to see Warwick alive and humbled, as opposed to dead and martyred. At some point he would have had to die but, preferably for the Yorkists, at a time and in a manner of his pupil's own choosing.

Montagu is credited by the *Arrivall* as having been slain 'in playne battayle', although Warkworth suggests that he may have been murdered on Warwick's orders. According to the latter version, Montagu was 'agreyde and apoyntede' with Edward, and even wore Yorkist colours beneath his own livery, ready to commit himself when the time was right. One of Warwick's men who had been assigned to keep an eye on him, catching Montagu in the act of declaring for Edward, 'felle uppone hyme, and kyllede hym'.

The Earl of Oxford made good his escape and fled to Scotland. The Duke of Exeter, stripped and left for dead, lay dangerously wounded throughout much of the day. At length he was taken to the nearby house of one of his servants, where he was tended by a surgeon.

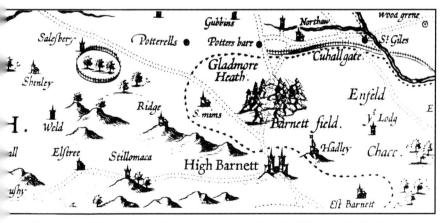

The Battle of Barnet. Detail from a map of Hertfordshire, probably by Woutneel, c1602.

Exeter was comparatively fortunate in that he had loyal friends and funds to secure medical treatment. It was not unusual for surgeons and other practitioners of sorts to be on hand to care for such as the duke, but the wounds of the rank and file generally remained untended. The Yorkist victors would have robbed the dead and dying, with the good people of Barnet emerging from their homes to pick over whatever might remain. The wounded who could crawl away sought shelter in surrounding woodland and in North Mimms and other nearby villages.

A letter written by Gerhard von Wesel, a Hanse merchant present in London, speaks of the wounded survivors of the battle as being hurt mostly in the lower portion of the body and in the face, some having lost their noses. In other words, their armour had succeeded in protecting them from fatal wounds, enabling them to emerge with their lives, but with such horrific injuries that, as von Wesel adds, they felt obliged to stay indoors, away from the gaze of the morbidly curious. The most seriously wounded who were unable to extricate themselves from the battlefield would have been buried with the dead. Some of the more celebrated casualties were removed, to be interred in various churches in London, but the common soldiers were thrown into burial pits, probably situated in an area to the north of the site known as 'Deadman's Bottom'. The number of dead stood at something in excess of a thousand. The toll might have been less but for the fact that Edward had instructed his men to give no quarter. The total included about 400 Yorkists, among whom 'were slayne in the filde the Lorde Cromwell, the Lord Saye, the Lord Mountjoies sonne and heyre, and many othar good Knyghts'. Edward ordered a chapel to be constructed near the battle site, a priest being appointed to say mass for the souls of the slain.

Right: Effigies of Sir John Mordaunt (d1504) and his wife Edith Latimer Turvey. Sir John fought in the battles of Barnet, Bosworth and at Stoke in 1487. Around his neck he wears the Lancastrian livery collar of SSs.
GEOFFREY WHEELER

The Madness of King Henry VI

King Henry VI is often presented as a feeble-minded individual, an object of imbecilic docility, increasingly dominated by a scheming, shrewish queen. In fact it is possible that he suffered from catatonic schizophrenia, a condition marked by symptoms of extreme withdrawal which, in his case, amounted to a total stupor.

Henry's health, both physical and mental, seems to have raised no cause for concern during his childhood. As a young man, however, he was noted for his otherworldliness, piety and, indeed, lethargy, as far as his involvement in affairs of state was concerned. He became ill quite unexpectedly in August 1453 while he was staying at Clarendon Palace, near Salisbury. The breakdown may have resulted from a sudden shock, coupled with despondency over England's ultimate defeat in the Hundred Years' War, by which all

The Hotel Dieu in Paris, a medieval hospital which opened in 1452 as home to the physicians of the French monarch, Charles VII.

her Continental possessions, except Calais, were lost. He was taken to Windsor Castle, where he spent much of the next eighteen months in seclusion. Both physically and mentally unresponsive to any stimulation, even the birth of his son – conceived before the illness came upon him – left him unmoved.

There was much talk of the illness which had afflicted his maternal grandfather, Charles VI of France, who had died insane. Charles had lost his reason in 1392, when he fell into a coma after having unaccountably attacked four of his own attendants. For the next thirty years his behaviour had oscillated between abnormal passivity and impulsive aggression. As with Henry, it is impossible to identify his condition, but he may have been suffering from porphyria, a hereditary disease involving much physical pain, weakness of the limbs and sensory deprivation.

Whereas the doctors of Charles VI had tried a number of novel treatments, which included drilling holes in his skull, Henry's medical advisers wisely limited themselves to recommending a special diet. It seemed to work, because by Christmas 1454 his condition had improved. In a letter to John Paston I, Edmund Clere wrote:

> *Blessid be God, the Kyng is wel amendid, and hath ben syn Cristemesday... . And in the Moneday after noon the Queen came to hym and brought my lord Prynce with here; and then he askid what the princes name was, and the Queen told him Edward; and than he hild vp his handes and thankid God therof. And he seid he neuer knew him til that tyme, nor wist not what was seid to him, nor wist not where he had be whils he hath be seke til now.*

While Henry may have returned to consciousness, there is evidence to suggest that any recovery was only partial. For example, the following May, when he was assaulted during the First Battle of St Albans, he is said to have retaliated only by rebuking his assailants: 'Foresothe, foresothe, ye do fouly to smyte a Kynge enoynted so.' He owed his life to his attendants, who carried him from the scene of action.

Henry's initial collapse had occasioned the appointment, in April 1454, of Richard, Duke of York, as Lord Protector, a post he was compelled to relinquish in February 1455 when Henry's health improved. York's reappointment in November 1455 coincided with a relapse in the king's condition, and lasted until February 1456 when, once again, Henry was reported to be on the mend. It seems that provided he was not comatose, he was considered fit for duty. The truth is that five and a half centuries on it is impossible to ascertain the state of Henry's mind at any given time. It was difficult enough for his contemporaries to make a judgement, with the Lancastrians trying to convince everyone that he was *compos mentis*, and the Yorkist lobby simultaneously seeking to depict him as being unfit to govern.

It is tempting to argue that after 1453 Henry was no more than a pawn in the Yorkist-Lancastrian struggle for power, but pawns can be sacrificed, and until 1471 – when Edward IV consolidated his own position – all parties had their reasons for keeping him alive. What can be said with certainty is that a strong monarch, either by force or statesmanship, could have averted a major conflict, but that with Henry's decline into madness civil war became inevitable.

King Edward IV leaving London with Henry VI (mounted) as hostage. From the painting 'London trained bands marching to Barnet' by J H Anschwitz, Royal Exchange mural, London.
GEOFFREY WHEELER

Chapter Five

THE BATTLE OF BARNET: THE AFTERMATH

EDWARD MAY OR MAY NOT have tried to save Warwick's life. Privately, he must have been pleased that his mentor was dead, for what could he have done with him? In all likelihood, had Warwick been taken alive he would have been confined to the Tower, to be disposed of in due course. Instead, Edward was free to wax lyrical about the qualities of a worthy foe. The corpse was kept intact – not for sentimental reasons but because, in accordance with established practice, Edward wished to put it on display so that all could see for themselves that the great man was no more. For two days, therefore, the bodies of both Warwick and Montagu were exhibited at St Paul's in case, as the *Arrivall* puts it, 'feyned seditiows tales' should assert that they were yet 'on lyve'. Afterwards their remains were laid to rest in the family mausoleum, Bisham Abbey.

Edward may have triumphed, but it had been a near run thing. Save for the mist, which had worked in his favour, his own cadaver could have been the one on public view. He could justly claim to be the conqueror of Warwick, but even this must be qualified, for Warwick's military record does not bear close scrutiny. He had contributed to the Duke of York's victory at the First Battle of St Albans in 1455; at Ludford Bridge, in 1459, he fled; a victory at Northampton in 1460 owed more to betrayal than military prowess; in 1461 he was soundly defeated at the Second Battle of St Albans. In short, Warwick was not one of the great generals of his time.

At a distance in time of 500 years it is difficult to comprehend the extraordinary impression Warwick made on his own age. Although the foundation of his strength lay in the titles and estates he had inherited, it was his outstanding ability which enabled him to create for himself a unique position as 'kingmaker'. Charismatic and a respected diplomat skilled in the arts of persuasion, he possessed an uncanny ability to sense the mood of popular feeling in the country. Living ostentatiously, he knew how to impress the common man and ruled England competently as long as Edward allowed him to do so.

At the very moment Warwick received his deathblow, Margaret of Anjou, Prince Edward and an assortment of Lancastrian exiles were heading across the Channel for Weymouth. The party landed towards the end of the day and made their way inland. At Cerne Abbey, Margaret received the news of Warwick's defeat and was for turning back. However, she was won over by her supporters, who assured her that the Lancastrians were 'never the febler' for the loss of one battle 'but rathar strongar', encouraging her in the belief that her presence would, in itself, guarantee a wealth of support. There was something in this argument, for it is one of the great wonders of the Wars of the Roses that no sooner had either side suffered a crushing defeat than it was back in the field with a new army.

Edward, too, had the problem of raising a new army to meet this fresh challenge. As Margaret would be approaching from the south-west he chose to muster his force to the west of London, at Windsor. The Lancastrians found that the counties of Somerset, Dorset and Wiltshire had been bled dry by Warwick, although they succeeded in raising the 'hoole myghte' of Devon and Cornwall. Methodically, they progressed to Taunton, Glastonbury, and Wells, 'hovinge in the contrye' in their efforts to recruit. The plan was to join forces with Jasper Tudor in Wales, but in an attempt to mislead Edward riders were despatched to Shaftesbury and Salisbury to spread false reports that they intended to advance on London at once.

Despite claims in the *Arrivall* that, being well supplied with reliable intelligence, Edward was not taken in, he could not be sure of Margaret's intentions. Perhaps mindful of the way in which he himself had profited by Warwick's inactivity, however, he resolved to take the fight to the enemy. Accordingly he left Windsor on 24 April, reaching Abingdon on the 27th, where he rested. On the 29th he marched to Cirencester, where he learned that Margaret was, in fact, en route to Bath. As at Barnet, he forced his army out of the town, making camp in the fields. The next day, with Margaret still not in view, he advanced to Malmesbury, where he heard that she had fallen back on Bristol.

On 2 May Edward received word that the Lancastrian army had been 'refreshed and relevyd' at Bristol and that, ready for action, it was drawing up on Sodbury Hill, 13 miles to the north-west of the city. Yet, once again, the information proved to be false, for Margaret intended to march on Gloucester. Coming into possession of this latest piece of information, Edward sent riders to warn Sir Richard Beauchamp, his constable at Gloucester, to hold the town at all costs. Beauchamp obeyed and when, at around 10.00 am on 3 May after an all-night march, the Lancastrians appeared before

Gloucester, hoping for a rapturous welcome and subsequent safe passage across the River Severn, they found the gates closed against them. Afraid to linger with Edward approaching, the weary host had to struggle on another ten miles to Tewkesbury, which they reached about 4.00 pm, having covered the forty-four miles from Bristol at a single march.

By this time each side was well aware of the other's location, for Edward had been shadowing the exhausted Lancastrians' progress throughout the day. The latter knew that he would soon be upon them, but in the absence of a bridge to cross the Severn they decided to make a stand,

> 'to abyde there th'aventure that God would send them'. They thererefore 'pight them in a fielde, in a close even at the townes end; the towne and the abbey at theyr backs; afore them and upon every hand of them fowle lanes, and depe dikes, and many hedges, with hylls and valleys; a ryght evill place to approache as cowlde well have been devysed.'

Undeniably, the Lancastrian position on the high ground at Gupshill, a mile to the south of the town, was a good defensive site, but by his determination to take the fight to them Edward ensured that the hunters had become the hunted. With the River Avon to the west, the River Swilgate to the east and Swilgate Brook to their rear, the

Sir James Ramsay's interpretation of the Battle of Tewkesbury.

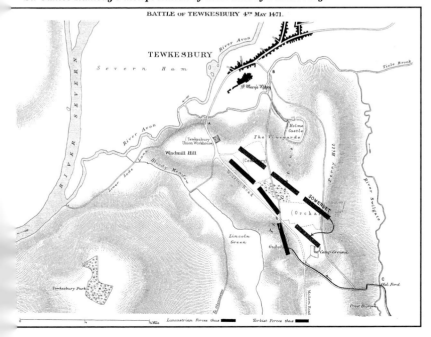

Lancastrians were effectively boxed in. It would be a case of victory or annihilation.

On Saturday 4 May Edward appeared, advancing upon the Lancastrians in three divisions, his van being led by Gloucester, the centre by himself, and the rear by Hastings. For the Lancastrians, Somerset, leading the vanguard, was posted on the left. The Prince of Wales with Lord Wenlock and Sir John Langstrother commanded the centre, with the Earl of Devon on the right. A little way to the right of the Lancastrian position there was a wood, and in order to guard against the possibility of an ambush Edward sent 200 spearmen to hold it.

Following a preliminary exchange of arrows and artillery fire, Gloucester attacked the Lancastrians. Unable to force their lines, he retreated. Whether through necessity or purpose, he succeeded with this manoeuvre in drawing Somerset from his entrenched position. Descending 'asyde-hande of the Kynges vawarde, and, by certayne pathes and wayes', Somerset closed with Edward's right flank. Edward turned his men to receive the charge, while Gloucester launched a counter-attack. The 200 spearmen emerged from their place of concealment on Somerset's left and he was routed, his men taking flight through vineyards towards the town. Edward then pushed into the Lancastrian position by the way left open by Somerset, and it was all over, the slope of the ground being now in his favour. The remaining Lancastrians fled in all directions. Many were drowned, 'namely at a mylene in the medowe fast by the towne', while those on the extreme right made for the Avon, only to be caught in a narrow meadow, still known as 'Bloody Meadow' as a result of the slaughter which took place there. Devon and Wenlock died fighting. Prince Edward was taken 'fleinge to the towne wards, and slayne in the fielde', possibly at Edward's command.

Entering the town, Edward went straight to the abbey church which was packed with trembling sanctuary-seeking Lancastrian fugitives. The rank and file were granted clemency, even though, the *Arrivall* states, there never had 'at any tyme bene grauntyd, any fraunchise to that place for any offendars agaynst theyr prince having recowrse thethar'. The legality of the situation depended, of course, upon Edward's right to call himself 'prince', but the priests, deciding that the better part of valour is discretion, chose not to argue the point. Therefore Edward's indulgence was not extended to the Lancastrian leaders, who were hauled out for judgement.

On 6 May the Duke of Somerset, Sir John Langstrother, Sir

The enthronement of Elizabeth Woodville as Edward IV's queen at Reading Abbey, September 1464. Although Warwick is depicted as honouring the occasion he was angered that he had lost face, as he had been negotiating for a French marriage.

Animosity and resentment grew as members of the queen's family began to receive privileges and honours. Here the royal family receive a present of a book from Anthony, second Earl Rivers, brother of Queen Elizabeth. The seeds were being sown for Warwick's defection.

Louis XI of France presents a contrite Warwick to Margaret of Anjou. She had agreed to see her old enemy, who had deserted the cause of Edward IV, but made him wait some time on his knees. GEOFFREY WHEELER

Prior to the Battle of Barnet three brothers meet up, along with their standard bearers. The Duke of Clarence (black bull standard) is reconciled with his brother Edward IV (white rose in splendour). Richard Duke of Gloucester (white boar) looks on. GEOFFREY WHEELER

Richard Neville, 'The Kingmaker' coloured drawing from the Rous Roll. GEOFFREY WHEELER

The Duke of Clarence coloured drawing from the Rous Roll. GEOFFREY WHEELER

Garter Stall plate for Duke of Gloucester. GEOFFREY WHEELER

Garter Stall plate for William Lord Hastings. GEOFFREY WHEELER

The standard of Henry VI.

The standard of Richard Neville Earl of Warwick.

Banners of the Leaders at Barnet.

Earl of Warwick (killed)

Marquis of Montague (killed)

Duke of Exeter (wounded)

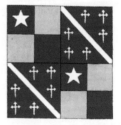

Earl of Oxford

Viscount Beaumont

Lord Cromwell (killed)

Edward IV

Duke of Clarence

Duke of Gloucester (wounded)

Lord Scales [Earl Rivers] (wounded)

Lord Hastings

Lord Saye (killed)

John de Vere Earl of Oxford. FREEZYWATER PUBLICATIONS

John Touchet Lord Audley. FREEZYWATER PUBLICATIONS

Detail showing the Battle of Barnet. GEOFFREY WHEELER

Death of the Earl of Warwick at the Battle of Barnet. GEOFFREY WHEELER

Warwick 'Kingmaker' memoralized in stained glass. To be seen at Cardiff Castle.
GEOFFREY WHEELER

8

Thomas Tresham, Sir Gervaise Clifton, Sir Hugh Courtenay, Sir Humphrey Audley, and ten or twelve others were brought before the Dukes of Gloucester and Norfolk – the Constable and Marshal of England respectively – and summarily condemned and executed. The bodies were spared the ignominy of 'dismembringe or settynge up', all being committed to decent burial. Margaret was not found at Tewkesbury. She had retired before the battle with the Princess of Wales and Lady Courtenay to a small House of Religion at some distance, probably Deerhurst, where she was found a few days later.

Advancing to Worcester on 7 May, Edward learned that the northern Lancastrians were arming. He turned to Coventry, calling for fresh levies, but the supply of Yorkist manpower had dried up. The day was saved by the Earl of Northumberland, who undertook to suppress all uprisings. To prove the peaceable state of the

Tewkesbury Abbey, scene of Edward IV's alleged abuse of the right of sanctuary claimed by defeated Lancastrians following the Battle of Tewkesbury.

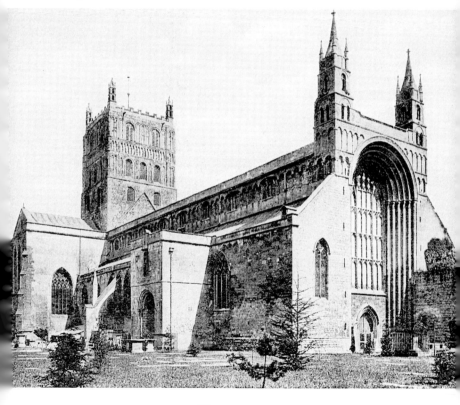

country, Northumberland came to Coventry with only a small following, 'and nat arrayed in manar of war'. Edward was relieved to accept his assurances, for trouble was brewing in the south.

Thomas Neville, called the Bastard of Fauconberg – an illegitimate son of William Neville, Earl of Kent – had been appointed Vice-Admiral by Warwick, with command of a fleet in the Channel. He decided to take advantage of Edward's absence from London to occupy the city and restore Henry. Having raised the nucleus of an army – some 300 men – at Calais, he landed in Kent on 5 May. A week later he reached London Bridge with ships and men and tried to effect a peaceful entry. When negotiations broke down, he marched away to cross the Thames at Kingston, with a view to storming London from the north. His intentions were thwarted by Anthony Woodville, Earl Rivers, who despatched some barges to block his advance. While Fauconberg retreated, messengers were sent to alert Edward.

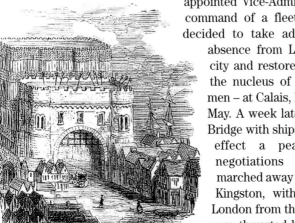

Traitors' Gate, London Bridge.
Thomas Neville, called the Bastard
of Fauconberg, attacked and burnt
this end of the bridge.

On 13 May Fauconberg opened a cannonade with guns landed from his ships, and burnt the Southwark end of London Bridge. The next day, with the aid of some rough and ready rebel supporters he had acquired in Essex, he launched assaults against Aldgate, Bishopsgate and the drawbridge in the middle of London Bridge. Defeated at all three points by stout resistance orchestrated by Earl Rivers, he withdrew to his ships moored at Blackwall, from where he crossed to Blackheath, remaining there three or four days, probably on Shooter's Hill, before his rag-tag army broke up, he himself retiring to Sandwich.

The House of Lancaster was in complete disarray. Had Fauconberg, Margaret and Warwick combined their resources, the year 1471 would have witnessed the premature end of the rival dynasty. Divided, they had fallen. Even Jasper Tudor had not arrived in time to help Margaret at Tewkesbury. After the battle, pursued by Edward's Welsh supporters, he fell back on Chepstow, and then Pembroke. At last he sailed from Tenby for France, with his nephew

Henry, Earl of Richmond, in tow. Forced by bad weather to land in Brittany, they were sheltered by Duke Francis II, and were largely forgotten. On Tuesday 21 May Edward entered London once more. Margaret of Anjou, who had been brought to him at Coventry, was included in the procession, like a prize exhibit in a Roman triumph.

Fauconberg's failure sealed Henry's fate, since it was realised that for as long as he lived he would constitute a focal point for Lancastrian disaffection. According to tradition, between 11.00 pm and midnight on the evening of Edward's arrival in London he was killed in the Tower. At any rate, next morning his strongly guarded body – with only the face exposed to view – was exhibited at St Paul's. Both at the time and afterwards Gloucester's name was associated with the deed. On 24 May the body was taken to a temporary resting-place at Chertsey Abbey, to be moved eventually to St George's Chapel, Windsor.

Edward hurried into Kent to mete out punishment. Nicholas Faunt, the Mayor of Canterbury, and other leaders were executed. Fauconberg took to the sea, hovering about the coastline until he was apprehended and beheaded. The task of dealing with minor offenders was delegated to the Duke of Norfolk and the Earl of Essex. It is recorded that they 'satt uppone all Kent, Sussex and Essex that were at the Blackhethe, and uppone many othere that were noght there'. Rather than opting for more bloodshed, it was decided to levy crippling fines, down to the very poorest offenders who, in order to raise the paltry sum of a few shillings, were compelled to sell their clothes.

On 29 May Edward wrote to friends in Bruges to advise them that his authority was fully restored. A strong and ruthless monarch, he would reign for the next eleven years, his throne secure from friend and foe alike. All challenges to his rule would come from his own brothers. The threat from Clarence cannot have been entirely unexpected, but what would have been the king's thoughts had he known that, after his death, his trusted younger brother, Gloucester, whose loyalty was beyond question, would seize the crown for himself, putting to death Edward's own two young sons? Within two years of Gloucester's usurpation all that Edward had worked for would be lost, the Lancastrians triumphant and the House of York destroyed, the setting of the Yorkist sun signalling not just the end of a dynasty, but of the medieval age.

The Royal Coat of Arms of Edward IV.

Edward would rule for a further eleven years.

Acts of Attainder

An Act of Attainder was an Act of Parliament by which one or more persons were declared to be attainted (deprived of their rights) and their property confiscated. In an age when men fought for gain, an Act of Attainder was the means of rewarding one's supporters. During the Wars of the Roses, with the advantage swinging back and forth between York and Lancaster, Acts of Attainder became commonplace, with land and property continuously changing hands. The following extract is from the Act of Attainder passed against some of the Lancastrians who had taken part in the Battle of Barnet.

And also where John Veer late Erl of Oxford, late of Wyvenho is the counte of Essex Knyght, George Veer, late of the same toune Knyght, Thomas Veer late of the same touen Knyght, Robert Harlyston, late of Shymplyng in the counte of Suffolk, Squyer, William Godmanston, late of Bromle in the counte of Essex, Squyer, John Durraunt, late of Collewston in the counte of Northampton Yoman, and Robert Gybbon, late of Wyngfeld in the counte of Suffolk Squyer, in the solempne and high fest of Ester Day, the which was the XIIII day of Aprill, the Xith yere of the reigne of our said sovereigne liege Lord, at Barnet in the counte of Hertford, and there and thenne togider assembled theym, with grete multitude of his naturall liege Lord, his roiall persone then and there beying, and his baner displayed, endtendying traiterousle then and there the fynall distruction of his said moost roiall persone, purposyng to have distroyd' hym, and deposed hym of his roiall astate, corone and dignitee, and there and then falsle and traiterousle made and reared werre agayns his astate, sheddyng there the blode of grete nombre of his subgiettes; in the which bataill, it pleased Almyghty God to gyf hym victorie of his ennemyes and rebelles, and to subdue the effecte of their fals and traiterous purpose.

Chapter 6

EPILOGUE

EDWARD IV DIED ON 9 APRIL 1483. He was 40 years old. The cause of his death, following a short illness, is something of a mystery. A visiting Italian cleric, Dominic Mancini, claims that the king caught a chill during a fishing trip. The author of the *Crowland Chronicle* avers that Edward was unaffected by any known kind of disease, while Philip de Commines suggests a fit of apoplexy, brought on by the news of the marriage between Charles VIII of France and the daughter of the Duke of Austria. Less savoury suggestions include venereal disease, engendered by Edward's unceasing lasciviousness. In this connection, it may be relevant that the woman for whom he had risked everything, Elizabeth, was absent from his bedside. Although no one implies that his death was brought about by anything other than natural causes, it is not beyond the bounds of possibility that enemies resorted to poison to shorten a reign which bore no signs of drawing to a premature close.

Owing to Edward's generosity, **George, Duke of Clarence**,

Edward IV's final military triumph was against the Scots, with the capture of Berwick in 1482. Edward himself did not take the field – perhaps a sign that he was already in failing health – the conduct of the campaign being delegated to Gloucester. A portion of Berwick's town wall depicted in this Victorian illustration has survived.

fared well, becoming one of the wealthiest men in the country. Despite his good fortune he remained very touchy and prey to all manner of imagined slights. According to the *Crowland Chronicle* it was the Act of Resumption of 1476 which marked the beginning of the end for him. This piece of legislation, geared to replenish the depleted royal coffers, deprived Clarence of certain of his estates. In a typical fit of pique, he withdrew from Court. Shortly afterwards his wife, Isabella, died, an occurrence he attributed to sorcery practised by Queen Elizabeth. He was further chagrined by Edward's refusal to entertain his ambition to marry the daughter of Charles, Duke of Burgundy. When, against his wishes, two of his retainers were condemned to death on charges of plotting against Edward, he upbraided the king publicly.

Edward had had enough. Clarence was arrested on a charge of high treason, tried and sentenced to death. Initially, Edward balked at his brother's execution, but Clarence was eventually executed privately in the Tower on 18 February 1478. He was 39 years old. It was rumoured that he had been drowned in a barrel of malmsey wine – doubtless an instance of black humour, based on his well-known fondness for the bottle.

In 1472 **Richard, Duke of Gloucester**, was married to Anne Neville, widow of the Prince of Wales and co-heiress with her sister, Isabella, to the estates of her father, the Earl of Warwick. He was appointed Lieutenant-General of the North and Warden of the Scottish Marches, placing him in an immensely prestigious and powerful position. The young couple's 'official' residence was the late Lancastrian stronghold, Pontefract Castle, but their real home was Middleham Castle, where Gloucester had spent his formative years in the care of Warwick. Such was the trust placed in him by Edward IV that, in his will, the king nominated Gloucester 'Lord Protector' for the duration of the twelve-year-old Edward V's minority. The Duke Richard of this period seems far removed indeed from King Richard III, usurper of the throne and supposed murderer of the 'Princes in the Tower', a monstrous tyrant who would

Middleham Castle, favoured residence of Richard III.

meet his end at Bosworth in 1485.

Until Edward IV's death **William Hastings, first Baron Hastings**, served as Lord Chamberlain, a post in which he expected to continue. His hopes were dashed by Gloucester, who had him arrested during a Council meeting on 13 June 1483. Although it seems unlikely that he had been plotting against Gloucester as charged, it was enough that he would have opposed any attempt to remove the young Edward V. He may have been held in the Tower and it is just possible that a trial of sorts took place. According to tradition, however, he was beheaded in makeshift fashion (over a log) shortly after his arrest.

ward V and his
unger brother Richard.

Richard Duke of Gloucester. Did he become the heartless monster who had his nephews murdered?

Henry Holland, third Duke of Exeter, survived the wounds he sustained at Barnet. An ex-Constable of the Tower of London, he spent the next four years incarcerated within its walls. His wife,

Bosworth battlefield where the House of York was crushed on 22 August 1485.
Inset: Henry Tudor, victor at Bosworth and possible candidate for the murder of the boys.

Anne, was granted a divorce, enabling her to marry her lover, Thomas St Leger. In June 1475 Exeter was given his freedom to enable him to join Edward's expedition to France – only to drown en route, somewhere between Dover and Calais. Did he fall or was he pushed? If the latter, then Edward and St Leger – for whom Exeter's rehabilitation could have proved awkward – must be the chief suspects.

John de Vere, thirteenth Earl of Oxford, found his way to France and was encouraged by Louis XI to turn his hand to piracy against English ships. In May 1473 he tried something a little more ambitious, appearing off the Essex coast with a small squadron. Unable to effect a landing, he hovered about the south coast before eventually occupying St Michael's Mount in Cornwall. There he languished, under siege, until compelled to surrender. For the next ten years he remained a prisoner in the fortress of Hammes, near Calais. An early attempt at freedom – he leapt into the shallow moat – failed, but in 1484 he persuaded his keeper, Sir James Blount, to escape with him to the court of the exiled Henry Tudor. The latter's success at Bosworth and Stoke Field was, in large measure, due to Oxford's generalship. The Earl died in 1513, aged seventy.

In the wake of Barnet, **Anne Beauchamp, Countess of**

St Michael's Mount in Cornwall occupied and held by John de Vere, thirteenth Earl of Oxford. He was eventually starved into surrender. He later escaped and joined Henry Tudor.

Warwick – one of the most tragic unsung figures in this mosaic of corruption and betrayal – sought sanctuary at Beaulieu Abbey in Hampshire. Her lands were speedily confiscated and redistributed among the victors. John Paston II, writing in 1473, notes that 'the

Countess of Warwick is now out of Beverley [sic] sanctuary, and Sir James Tyrell conveyeth her northward, men say by the King's assent; whereto some men say that the Duke of Clarence is not agreed.' She was permitted to live in obscurity and died in 1492.

The ruins of Beaulieu Abbey where the Countess of Warwick sought sanctuary following the death of her husband at Barnet.

Queen Margaret of Anjou was confined to the Tower until 1476, when she was ransomed by Louis XI for the queenly sum of 50,000 crowns. She was given a pension of 6,000 livres and spent the rest of her days in a small château in Anjou, dying there in 1482.

For a short time **Elizabeth Woodville** was the Queen Mother. Then Gloucester produced evidence which proved – to his own satisfaction – that the marriage of Elizabeth and Edward had been illegal, Edward having already been betrothed to Lady Eleanor Butler. Their offspring, he argued, were therefore illegitimate. Gloucester's apologists argue that, having successfully disinherited Edward V, he would have had nothing to gain by murdering him. Indulging in a little skulduggery of her own, Elizabeth agreed to marry her eldest daughter, Elizabeth of York, to Henry Tudor if he could successfully dethrone Gloucester – now Richard III. Upon Henry's accession to the throne in 1485, the position of Elizabeth Woodville and her surviving

A Victorian artist's impression of Elizabeth Woodville who agreed to marry her eldest daughter, Elizabeth of York, to Henry Tudor.

Coat of Arms of Elizabeth Woodville.

children was again legitimized. Elizabeth became Queen Dowager, living on until 1492.

By marrying Elizabeth of York, Henry VII hoped to unite the Houses of Lancaster and York, bringing the Roses conflict to a final conclusion. The Yorkist revolt of 1487, resulting in the Battle of Stoke Field, prompted him to make arrangements for Elizabeth of York's coronation. It was a symbolic gesture, Henry himself declining to take part in the ceremony.

Chapter Seven

EXPLORING THE BATTLEFIELD

T HE BEST WAY TO REACH the battlefield is via High Barnet station on the Northern Line of London's underground train system. By road, an approach can be made via Junction 23 of the M25 and the A1081 St Albans Road. The battlefield area is contained almost within a single square (2497) of Ordnance Survey Explorer 173: London North. A street atlas is a far more useful guide.

A good starting point for any exploration of the battlefield is Barnet Museum, located at 31 Wood Street – by the bus stop opposite Barnet Church. This contains a model of the battle, together with useful maps and publications. Cannonballs unearthed on the battlefield from time to time are also housed here, but although the local press tends to associate these with the Battle of Barnet they are invariably of a much later date and were deposited by accident rather than by design. Indeed, as curator and local historian John Heathfield points out, archaeological investigation has failed to uncover any relics which can definitely be associated with the battle.

Battle of Barnet 500th Anniversary Exhibition Model 1971.
GEOFFREY WHEELER

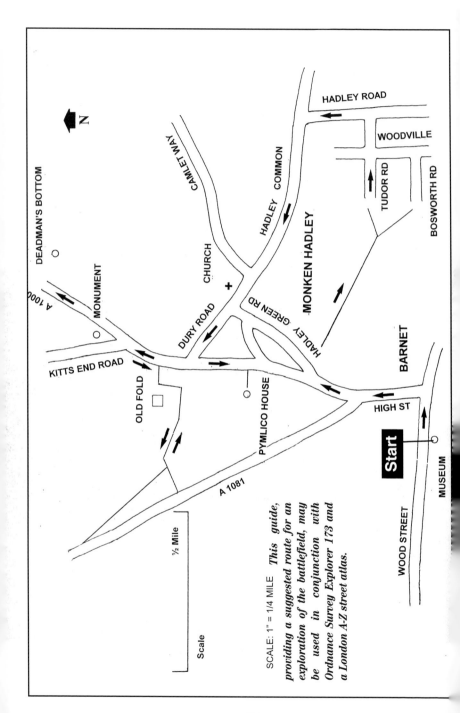

SCALE: 1" = 1/4 MILE *This guide, providing a suggested route for an exploration of the battlefield, may be used in conjunction with Ordnance Survey Explorer 173 and a London A-Z street atlas.*

½ Mile

Scale

The area in the vicinity of Wood Street and its junction with the High Street prescribes the limits of old Barnet upon which the Yorkist left wing, hotly pursued by the Lancastrian right, fell back. From Wood Street, turn left into Barnet High Street and continue walking – the landscape opening out as you approach Monken Hadley and Barnet High Street develops into the old Great North Road. The junction with Hadley Green Road may well define the Yorkist lines – Hastings to the left and Edward IV to the right. An information board on the west side of Hadley Green Road identifies the possible Yorkist and Lancastrian positions.

Take the public footpath opposite, which stretches away to the south-east. Immediately, you become aware of the eminence occupied by Barnet – something which you will already have noticed if you approached the town from the underground station.

Looking towards London along the public footpath opposite Hadley Green information board, marking the Yorkist centre ground.

(On clear days the Post Office Tower is visible on the skyline.) Also of interest is the uneven nature of the ground, falling away through the trees. Cross the final field to emerge on Bosworth Road. At the end of Bosworth Road, turn left into Woodville, right into Latimer Road, and left into Hadley Road.

A left turn at the top of Hadley Road brings you on to Hadley Common and the rear of Gloucester's position. His 'battle' would have straddled the present day road at a point to the south of its junction with Camlet Way. To the right, the ground drops away sharply – an unfriendly feature with which Gloucester had to contend in his advance on Exeter's position. Beyond the Camlet Way junction, by the roadside, there once stood a tree known as 'Warwick's Oak' – one alleged location of the earl's death.

A little further on, to the right, is St Mary's Church, dating from 1494. An ecclesiastical structure had existed at least 200 years before this, for a list of rectors in the porch begins at 1244. As early as 1136, however, a Benedictine monastery was established at Walden in Essex, and within the terms of its endowment a hermitage was constructed at Hadley – hence the appellation 'Monken Hadley'. At an indeterminate date the hermitage was replaced or supplemented by a church which survived until the construction of St Mary's.

St Mary's Church, Monken Hadley.

The most curious feature of the church is the beacon affixed to the top of the tower. According to the antiquarian John Stow, the Earl of Warwick lit the church beacon the night before the Battle of Barnet as a guide to those of his supporters who were still arriving. It is probable that the beacon on Hadley church was, indeed, used as a guide for travellers crossing Enfield Chase – just as a light was kept burning in the tower of All Saints Church in York to guide wayfarers through the Forest of Galtres – but if Warwick did light a beacon, then it must have been

King Edward IV, Oak, Hadley Wood

Edwardian photograph of 'Warwick's Oak' (labelled 'King Edward IV Oak'), one suggested location for Warwick's death.

A Victorian interpretation of the death of Warwick. Shields were not being used by this time.

GEOFFREY WHEELER

Victorian engraving of Monken Hadley's church tower and its prominent beacon.

situated on the current building's predecessor.

From St Mary's, walk on into Dury Road. The junction of Dury Road with the Great North Road may mark Montagu's position. Exeter's battle would have stretched away to the right. Turn to the right, into Hadley Highstone. At the junction of Hadley Highstone and Kitts End Road is the battlefield monument-cum-milestone, Hadley High Stone. The main inscription reads: 'Here was fought the famous battle between Edward the 4th and the Earl of Warwick April the 14th ANNO 1471 in which the Earl was defeated and slain.' It was erected in 1740 by Sir Jeremy Sambrooke, the owner of 'Gobions', an estate two miles (3.2km) to the south-east of North Mimms, which lies on the Great North Road (A1000) between

Junction of Dury Road and Hadley Highstone, defining the Lancastrian centre ground.

Hadley memorial to the Battle of Barnet erected by Jeremy Sambrooke in 1740.

Detail of wording on the stone memorial at Hadley.
GEOFFREY WHEELER

Potters Bar and Hatfield. Originally the column stood near a public house called the 'Two Brewers', before being relocated a century later. In the popular imagination, its present location has become identified as the site of Warwick's death.

One of the many problems of the battlefield does concern the location of the dead. No burial pits have been found for the thousand or so fighting men who were killed in the battle. The remains of individuals of social significance were removed for burial, and it may well be that other corpses were interred in the churchyards at Monken Hadley and Barnet. This happened after the Battle of Towton (1461), when a number of victims were deposited in the churchyard of All Saints, Saxton. Even so, burial pits have been unearthed at Towton, and they must exist at Barnet.

One possible location is 'Deadman's Bottom'. Most maps put this feature well to the north of the battlefield (OS Explorer 173 255989), although it is occasionally marked a little nearer. At the point on the Great North Road where the houses on the right finish, the land dips sharply towards Hadley Wood. One can envisage a scenario in which fleeing Lancastrians were cut off here, surrounded and butchered. As for Warwick, if he met his death in the thick of the fighting then it would probably have occurred to the south of Hadley High Stone, whereas if he was killed in flight this would have happened further afield.

In recent years the Chipping Barnet Heritage Trust has been working with the sculptor John Somerville (a resident of Barnet) with a view to the creation of a new battlefield memorial. According to press reports, the scheme is faltering over the issue of a suitable site. Although Wood Street has been suggested, a more appropriate location would be Hadley Green.

From Hadley High Stone, walk back down the Great North Road

One of the suggested locations of 'Dead Man's Bottom', to the north-east of Hadley Highstone.

as far as Old Fold Lane and Old Fold Manor Golf Course, which marks Oxford's position. The current Old Fold Manor is eighteenth century in origin. At the time of the battle its moated predecessor was owned by the Frowyk family. The three-sided moat is the only feature of the battlefield which has remained essentially unchanged throughout the centuries, and this has tempted historians to assign it an importance which may be unwarranted.

At the end of Old Fold Lane, turn sharp left on to the public footpath and continue walking until you reach a junction. The main (centre) path terminates at Sunset View, off St Albans Road (A1081),

Entrance to the present-day Old Fold Manor. Warwick may have used the medieval manor as a command post.

while the path to the left leads to Hadley Green West. Take the path on the right, leading across Old Fold Manor Golf Course. As you emerge from the trees the Club House – with dry moat to its rear – is visible to the right. The area is littered with scraps of hedgerows and thickets, yet Alfred Burne in The Battlefields of England claims that the hedge 'behind which part of the Lancastrian army lay is still in existence and can be identified'.

Initially, it seems absurd to attempt to match a hedge that exists today with one which existed in the fifteenth century. Allowing for gaps, Burne identifies the hedge – and an accompanying ditch – as the one 'running from the moat ... thence along the top of the ridge, and dropping down gradually to the modern St Albans road'. Apparently, dating tests have been carried out which tend to confirm its great age.

Follow the (poorly marked) public footpath across the golf course until you reach a junction. Instead of continuing on to St Albans Road, branch off to the right and follow the path along the ridge. This route terminates a little further up St Albans Road. According to Burne, Oxford's 'battle' was deployed on this NW-SE axis.

The most intriguing questions about Old Fold Manor are posed by Frederick Cass in a paper produced for the London and Middlesex

Old Fold golf course is littered with shrubbery and hedges, making it difficult to establish which (if any) may have provided cover for the Lancastrian army.

The St Albans Road terminus (OS Explorer 173 238981) of the longer public footpath which traverses Old Fold golf course.

Approaching Old Fold golf course from the shorter public footpath to St Albans Road (OS Explorer 173 240977), to the rear of the Lancastrian right wing.

Pymlico House, Monken Hadley – alleged site of a vanished chapel, erected by the order of Edward IV in commemoration of those killed at the Battle of Barnet.

Archaeological Society in 1882.

It would be interesting to know, under what banner the inhabitants of Old Fold ranged themselves, and how it was occupied during the battle... . Did gallant soldiers issue from its gate to take their part in the fray? Did any wounded fugitive cross its moat, at the close of the engagement, to seek shelter or to die? Who can tell whether Warwick may not have established his head quarters within...?

Instead of emerging onto St Albans Road, retrace your steps through the golf course and back along Old Fold Lane, turning right into the Great North Road. Continue walking as far as Hadley Green West at the end of which is Pymlico House.

Following a decisive battle it was customary to make provision for a chapel – a place of prayer where mass could be said for the souls of the dead. Thus St Mary's Chapel in Wakefield is said to have been enriched by Edward IV in memory of his father and brother, killed at the battle in 1460. Similarly, before his death at Bosworth in 1485 Richard III endowed a chapel at Towton to commemorate those who fell there in 1461. It is believed that in the aftermath of the Battle of Barnet, Edward IV arranged for a chapel to be erected and for the appointment of a priest. There has been speculation that this chapel – if it existed – was situated on the site occupied by Pymlico House. Confirmation would also identify the location of any burial pits, which would have been close by. Others claim that St Mary's Church was built by Edward to serve this purpose.

So much of what we know about the Battle of Barnet is based upon surmise and legend. This becomes even more apparent as one explores the battlefield. At Wakefield and Towton, site exploration clarifies and elucidates; in contrast, at Barnet familiarity with the landscape tends to increase the uncertainty and compound the confusion.

The major primary source we have in helping us to fix the exact location is John Paston III, who remarked to his mother that the battle took place half a mile from Barnet. Was this an accurate assessment of the distance involved, or merely the rough guess of a wounded fugitive who feared for his life? And was the Duke of Somerset not present? Which wing of the Yorkist army was under Gloucester's command? Did Warwick die a hero's death?

Inevitably, during the walk back to Wood Street one is forced to

Did Warwick die a hero's death?
GEOFFREY WHEELER

Ring with the Warwick badge of the bear and ragged staff. It is said to have belonged to Richard Neville, Earl of Warwick.
GEOFFREY WHEELER

Margaret of Anjou

During the early years of Henry VI's reign it was inevitable that the rival factions at court should seek to influence the king's selection of a wife. The Yorkists favoured a choice between three princesses of Armagnac, but the scheme failed to materialize and the Beauforts proposed their own candidate – Margaret of Anjou. The father of the prospective fifteen-year-old bride, Duke René, insisted that the province of Anjou, which his family had owned before it had been overrun by the English in the ongoing Hundred Years' War, should be returned to him. Henry acceded to this condition, thus playing into the hands of the Yorkists who argued, with some justification, that Margaret came at too high a price. Nevertheless, in 1445 the marriage went ahead. The Beauforts had their new friend at court, while the Yorkists had a new enemy.

Margaret was noted for her beauty and charm, but as her husband's mental condition deteriorated she also began to display a strength of character which her sponsors had overlooked. Perhaps this quality led to her reputation as a warrior queen – a Boudicca-like figure leading her troops into battle. For example, in *The Battlefields of England*, Alfred Burne detects 'a feminine hand' in the manoeuvre resulting in the flank attack at the Second Battle of St Albans. In reality, however, her function was that of a figurehead and rallying point for Lancastrian sympathizers and, while it is often convenient to refer to 'Margaret's army', it is unlikely that she ever took an active part in campaign management.

Well before battle commenced, Margaret would retire to a safe distance. At the Second Battle of St Albans (1455) her army was probably commanded by Andrew Trollope. At Wakefield (1460) she was not present – although Shakespeare (*Henry VI Part III*) has her placing a paper crown upon the Duke of York's head before stabbing him. At Tewkesbury (1471) the Lancastrians were led by the Duke of Somerset, while Margaret herself sought premature sanctuary at nearby Deerhurst.

Henry VI's queen was simply a woman of her time: a pawn in the marriage stakes and little more than a pawn in the monumental power struggle which followed. The fact that, despite the disadvantages incurred by her gender, she was still able to command respect says much for her fighting spirit.

retreat into one's imagination, with the recognition that the place has the unique 'feel' of a battleground: sombre, melancholy – almost funereal. From Hastings to the Somme, the same sensation is experienced on all battlefields. You have only to close your eyes and you can see the Yorkist lines advance – yes, Gloucester is on the right wing – as the Lancastrians stand fast uttering defiant cries of 'A Warwick! A Warwick!' Gloucester succeeds in overcoming Exeter. On the Yorkist left, Oxford turns the irresolute Hastings, whose men are fleeing in terror. The armies, now locked together, are enveloped in the mist. Neither side is giving ground. At length, shadowy figures can be seen approaching from the south – friend or foe? It is difficult to tell. Yorkists, surely? Lancastrian archers fire a volley of arrows. But their targets are Oxford's men, who have regrouped. Naturally, Oxford suspects treachery, and he withdraws. Committing his reserve, Edward IV is now pressing forward into the thick of the fighting. The Lancastrian lines waver, 'Betrayal!' on the lips of every man. Somerset might have made a difference, but he is not here. Montagu is killed. Warwick is led away by his retainers, but the small group is surrounded and, one by one, the earl's men are cut down. Finally, Warwick himself falls – but where? The spot is obscured by the confusion of battle, the fifteenth-century landscape – so different from that of today – and the obstinate mist. Had it not been for the mist Warwick might have prevailed. One wonders whether he was aware of the derivation of the name of the place – Gladsmuir Heath – he had chosen for the battle. It means 'grey moor'.

Death of Warwick at Barnet by the late Peter Jackson.
GEOFFREY WHEELER

William Shakespeare and the Battle of Barnet

Shakespeare wrote for the Tudors. In this connection it is noteworthy that in order to secure favour at court, despite the elapse of so many years since the official end of the Wars of the Roses, the playwright found it expedient to discredit the Yorkists wherever possible. Throughout the relevant history plays, therefore, the Lancastrians are presented as heroic statesmen and the Yorkists as rapacious villains.

The Battle of Barnet is included in Act V, Scenes II and III, of *Henry VI Part III*. Scene II of the play ('A field of Battle near Barnet') opens with Edward IV entering with a wounded Earl of Warwick:

> *So, lie thou there: die thou, and*
> *die our fear;*
> *For Warwick was a bug that fear'd us all –*
> *Now, Montague, sit fast; I seek for thee,*
> *That Warwick's bones may keep thine company.*

Edward departs, leaving Warwick to deliver his final soliloquy:

> *For who liv'd king, but I could dig his grave?*
> *And who durst smile when Warwick bent his brow?*
> *Lo, now my glory smear'd in dust and blood!*
> *My parks, my walks, my manors that I had,*
> *Even now forsake me; and of all my lands*
> *Is nothing left me but my body's length!*
> *Why, what is pomp, rule, reign, but earth and dust!*
> *And, live we how we can, yet die we must.*

Before he expires, Oxford and Somerset – who was probably not present at Barnet – arrive to tell him that Montagu is dead and that Queen Margaret has landed. They remove Warwick's body, allowing Edward to re-enter in triumph:

> *Thus far our fortune keeps an upward course,*
> *And we are grac'd with wreaths of victory.*
> *But in the midst of this bright-shining day*
> *I spy a black, suspicious, threatening cloud,*
> *That will encounter with our glorious sun*
> *Ere he attain his easeful western bed.*

Edward, too, is aware of Margaret's arrival and the scene shifts to Tewkesbury.

Another version of the death of Warwick.

GEOFFREY WHEELER

92

Chapter Eight

FOLKLORE

O NE OF THE MOST POPULAR contemporary theories behind Edward IV's whirlwind courtship of Elizabeth Woodville concerned magic powers attributed to the bride's mother, Jacquetta of Luxembourg. The story has its origins in her family's somewhat rash claim to be descended from Medusina, a mythical creature variously described as a serpent-witch, water-nymph and mermaid.

According to the legend, the founder of Luxembourg, Count Siegfried of the Ardennes, married Medusina in the belief that she was no more than a beautiful woman. She agreed to be his wife on condition that for one day and night each month he must leave her to her own devices. Accordingly, once a month she would disappear into the network of tunnels beneath Siegfried's castle. At length Siegfried's curiosity overcame him and he followed her down – to find her reclining in a bath, a scaly fish tail hanging over the side. Her secret laid bare, so to speak, she leaped into the River Alzette and was never seen again.

Elizabeth Woodville.

To a superstitious medieval peasantry such twaddle added to the mystique of the ruling class, as well as providing the royal line with an additional, albeit tenuous, claim to legitimacy. At any rate, a neighbour of the Woodvilles, Thomas Wake of Blisworth in Northamptonshire, alleged that Jacquetta had used her skills as a witch, inherited from her fabulous forebear, to make Edward fall in love with Elizabeth. Wake claimed that Jacquetta had fashioned a lead model of Edward, which had been instrumental in her sorcery.

93

Wake's allegations must have made even the most sceptical citizen stop and think, for Edward's behaviour in the matter had been nothing short of extraordinary. A more prosaic explanation for the claim is that Wake was a supporter of the Nevilles. He went public with his story in 1469, soon after Edward's detention – when Warwick was searching for any information which might aid him in his efforts to discredit and destroy the Woodvilles.

Another curious legend surrounding the courtship of Edward and Elizabeth is that of the 'Queen's Oak' beneath which, supposedly, the couple first met. Standing near Potterspury Lodge in what was then the extensive Whittlebury Forest, the oak allegedly survived until 1997, when it was destroyed by fire. Prior to its demise, however, tests had been carried out which proved that the tree was no more than 340 years old, leaving it almost 200 years short of the age required to lend credibility to the story of its remarkable longevity.

If the black arts had their role to play in popular culture, so too did the concept of divine intervention. While he languished in exile, Edward allegedly 'prayed to God, owr Lady, and Seint George, and ... specially prayed to Seint Anne to helpe hym', promising that the next time he saw an image of Saint Anne he would 'make his prayers, and gyve his offeringe, in honor and worshipe of that blessyd Saynte.'

During his pause at Daventry in the course of his march to London, he attended the Palm Sunday parish church service, where, according to the Arrivall,

> God and Seint Anne, shewyd a fayre miracle; a good epronostique of good aventture that aftar shuld befall unto the Kynge by the hand of God, and mediation of that holy matron, Seint Anne.

Apparently, fixed to a pillar in the church was an alabaster image of Saint Anne,

> closed and clasped togethars with four bordes, small, payntyd, and gowynge rownd abowt the image, in manar of a compas, lyke as it is to see comonly, and all abowt, where was suche ymages be wont to be made for to be solde and set up in churches, chapells, drosses, and oratories, in many placis. And this ymage was thus shett, closed, and clasped, accordynge to the rulles that, in all the churches of England, be observyd, all ymages to be hid from Ashe Wednesday to Estarday in the mornynge. And

so the sayd ymage had bene from Ashwensday to that tyme.

Suddenly, the *Arrivall* continues,

the bords compassynge the ymage about gave a great crak, and a little openyd, which the Kynge well perceyveyd and all the people about hym. And, anon, aftar, the bords drewe and closed togethars agayne, withowt any mans hand, or touchinge, and, as thwoghe it had bene a thinge done with a violence, with a gretar might it openyd all abrod, and so the ymage stode, open and discovert, in syght of all the people there beynge.

Edward gave thanks for what he considered to be a good omen, a token of God's blessing on his venture. Then,

'remembringe his promyse, he honoryd God and Seint Anne, in that same place, and gave his offerings.' And of more importance, 'All thos, also, that were present and sawe this worshippyd and thanked God and Seint Anne.'

As with most omens, this one was capable of differing interpretations, a cracked image usually having more to do with bad luck. In this respect the incident may have something in common with William of Normandy's arrival at Pevensey Bay in 1066. When, on landing, the Conqueror tripped and fell flat on his face, he turned the situation to his advantage by announcing that he had already taken English soil in his hands. In the present case, it may be that the chance cracking of the image came first, with the story of the earlier vow hastily appended to transform an inauspicious sign into a glorious miracle.

Witchcraft again came to the fore in the events leading up to the arrest and execution of Clarence. Under torture, John Stacy, Fellow of Merton College, Oxford, incriminated himself, together with Thomas Blake, Chaplain of Merton College, and Thomas Burdet, a prominent West Midlands landowner, of imagining the death of Edward IV and Prince Edward by sorcery. Burdet had allegedly instructed Stacey and Blake, described as astronomers and necromancers, to 'calculate and work out the Nativities of the King and Prince of Wales', as a result of which the early deaths of Edward and his eldest son were predicted. The indictment against Burdet also claimed that he did 'falsely and treacherously disperse and disseminate divers seditious and treasonable bills, rhymes and ballads, containing complaints, seditions and treasonable arguments' against the king. Burdet and Clarence were friends, and the subsequent trial – which resulted in Burdet's execution – may well have been an attempt by the government to discredit the duke.

The prognostications of the not-so-wise men proved to be uncannily accurate, as did another prophecy which was doing the rounds at the time, and which Burdet may have been foolish enough to broadcast. It was said that Edward would be succeeded by someone whose name began with the initial 'G' – as, indeed, he was – but by Richard of Gloucester, not George, Duke of Clarence, who was widely perceived to constitute the real threat to stability.

Provided their practitioners were not working against you, the black arts were not entirely taboo. Thus, the fog which settled over

An artist's impression of Edward IV's brother, George, the Duke of Clarence.

96

the battlefield at Barnet was said to have been conjured up by Friar Bungay, specifically to aid the House of York. An historical figure, Bungay appears in two celebrated pieces of fiction: Robert Greene's play of 1592, *Friar Bacon and Friar Bungay* and Lord Lytton's historical novel, *The Last of the Barons*, published in 1843.

In Lytton's version of the Battle of Barnet in *The Last of the Barons*, Bungay (in the employ of Jacquetta of Luxembourg) serves as comic relief, producing the mist with the aid of an absurd incantation: 'Barabbarara, Santhinoa, Foggibus increscebo, confusio Garabbora, vapor et mistes!' In fact, Bungay had lived and died two centuries before the battle. Had Warwick emerged victorious, doubtless the fog would have been conjured up in aid of the Lancastrian cause.

Conspicuous by their absence at Barnet are battlefield ghosts. English Civil War battlefields are rich in ghostly phenomena, yet Wars of the Roses battlefields (with one or two exceptions) are singularly lacking in supernatural presences. The lack of ghosts at Barnet is all the more curious because neighbouring East Barnet is one of the most haunted spots in the country, Church Hill Road having been famously described as 'The Ghosts' Promenade', such is the volume of its spectral traffic. There have been sightings of a phantom knight in armour in Oak Hill Park, but this is believed to be the ghost of Geoffrey de Mandeville, whose sole tenuous connection with the Battle of Barnet is as founder of Walden Abbey and, as a consequence, Monken Hadley church.

Seeking Sanctuary

Throughout the Wars of the Roses, prominent Yorkists and Lancastrians alike sought sanctuary – which is to say, when pursued by their enemies they claimed the protection of the church.

The right of sanctuary in England was introduced by King Ethelbert around AD 600. In order to claim sanctuary, a fugitive might have to seize hold of a sanctuary knocker on a church door, or, perhaps, sit on a particular chair – the 'frith stool' – beside the altar. Sometimes, as at Beverley and Hexham, it was sufficient to reach a safe zone, extending a mile beyond the church, a series of stone sanctuary crosses marking the outer boundary. Sanctuary could be claimed for a limited period only. After forty days a felon would have to emerge and confess his crime, after which he was sent into exile.

Although the sanctuary system worked pretty well it was not foolproof, depending as it did on a set of common rules based on the universal acceptance of the sanctity of consecrated ground. Places of worship – particularly the great abbeys and monasteries, by virtue of their wealth – were often considered fair game in times of war, so throughout the Middle Ages the Scots and English desecrated each other's religious houses at will. In 1322, for example, the army of Edward II plundered the monasteries of Holyrood, Melrose and Dryburgh, slaughtering the monks in the process. In return, the Scots sacked the abbeys of Byland and Rievaux and burned churches and monasteries as far south as Beverley.

Also in 1322, following his defeat at the Battle of Boroughbridge, the rebel Earl of Lancaster had sought sanctuary in the chapel in the town's market square. It did him little good, for he was removed and taken away for trial and execution. His enemies were probably acting within the letter of the law, for whereas all churches afforded protection to common felons, only a limited number were licensed, under Royal Charter, to give sanctuary to political refugees.

In reality the situation often lacked clarity. In 1471, after the execution of Lancastrian nobles who had taken refuge in Tewkesbury Abbey church, it was considered necessary to rededicate the church, suggesting that an act of sacrilege had taken place even though, in terms of sanctuary law, it did not enjoy political refugee status. At times a decision on whether to grant sanctuary might be made by the head of a religious house. The Yorkist pretender, Perkin Warbeck, twice sought sanctuary. On the run in 1497, he arrived at Beaulieu Abbey, but the abbot betrayed him and Warbeck was arrested. At large again in 1498, he threw himself on the mercy of the prior of Sheen Abbey – who promptly informed Henry VII of the fugitive's arrival.

The most celebrated sanctuary was that afforded by Westminster Abbey. In 1470, when Queen Elizabeth fled there, she was treated with magnanimity by the Earl of Warwick, who ensured that she was comfortably provided for. In 1483, when Gloucester seized the crown, Elizabeth hurried to Westminster once more. On this occasion she was less fortunate, for Gloucester proceeded to lay siege to the sanctuary, forcing Cardinal Bouchier to persuade Elizabeth to deliver the Duke of York into Gloucester's hands.

In short, sanctuary was the very last resort of the most desperate of fugitives.

Saxon chapel at Deerhurst Abbey. Queen Margaret may have sought sanctuary here before the Battle of Tewkesbury.

Chapter Nine

ARTICLES OF WAR

C ANNON WERE FIRST USED in England in 1327 by Edward III, in his wars against Scotland. Very large cannon were available by the mid-fifteenth century, when, for example, Mons Meg – weighing over 4 tons (4,000kg) and with a calibre of 20ins (50cm) – was made for James II of Scotland. (An enthusiastic gunner, James was killed by an exploding cannon in 1460.) However, the artillery used by Edward and Warwick at Barnet would have been much lighter – probably bastard culverins firing 7lb (3kg) stone balls.

According to the Warkworth Chronicle, the 300 mercenaries who accompanied Edward to England in 1471 all possessed 'hande-gonnes'. Although the actual numbers do not agree, this is confirmed by Holinshed's statement that, upon his arrival in London, Edward had 'five hundred smokie gunners marching foremost, being strangers, of such as he had brought over with him'.

The term 'hande-gonnes' probably refers to the hand culverin which comprised an iron barrel, with a bore of three-quarters of an inch (2cm), attached to a straight piece of wood. Weighing up to 16lbs (7kg), it was fired from a rest and required two men for its management. Slow and inaccurate at the best of times, the handgun, in its embryonic stages, was notoriously unreliable. As Charles Ashdown has remarked in *European Arms and Armour*, it is a wonder that they were used at all.

On expansive, open battlefields such as Towton (1461), the longbow still ruled. Traditionally, the best longbows were made of yew, many staves being imported from Spain and Italy. However, foreign merchants responded to the surge in demand resulting from the Wars of the Roses by increasing their prices, so that by 1471 inferior home-grown wood was being substituted for the quality product. But Barnet was not the open plain of Agincourt, and the mist which rendered artillery redundant also hampered the archers. We do know that John Paston III was wounded in the right elbow by an arrow, and the Lancastrian archers were responsible for the friendly fire which sent Oxford's men running from the field. In this respect, at least, the longbow did decide the outcome.

Despite the claims of some revisionist historians, medieval armour was heavy and knights and men-at-arms wielding swords in sustained combat soon became exhausted. For this reason there would often be a lull in the fighting to enable the participants to regain their strength.

At Barnet, a battle consisting almost exclusively of close-quarter, hand-to-hand combat, a far more significant weapon was the steel blade. At the top end of the range was the long sword. Weighing in at anything up to 4lbs (1.8kg) and with a length of up to 43ins (109cm), it was essentially a two-handed weapon, requiring strength – and space – for effective use. Of greater value in close combat were the short sword and the dagger. The short sword, around 24ins (61cm) long, could be held close to the body, while the dagger, up to 18ins (46cm) in length and with a slender blade, was capable of being honed to a much finer point. Together, dagger and short sword formed a potent cocktail of death.

The cramped nature of the field of battle, with the overlap of the opposing lines and the added presence of fog, meant that there was little scope for the use of tactics which might normally be expected to turn the fighting in one's favour. Heavy cavalry became a liability. In a confused mêlée, the isolated mounted knight became an easy target for foot soldiers. Once unhorsed and prostrate on the ground, he was helpless. Assailants could raise his visor and attack his exposed face with short sword and dagger. Even as a means of effecting an escape a horseman's charger could prove a hindrance, for what it might gain in strength and durability it lost in fleetness of hoof. (Revisionist historians who suggest that generously armoured horsemen were more agile than we were once led to believe would do well to put their theories to a personal test.)

In response to the steady expansion of bone-crunching weaponry, the period of the Wars of the Roses witnessed corresponding developments in the sophistication of body armour. Whereas a knight or man-at-arms would be encased in plate armour, the common soldier had to make do with much less personal protection. He would have been provided with a metal helmet and possibly armour to protect part of his face and neck, while body protection would have consisted of a padded tunic bearing the coat of arms of his master, perhaps worn in conjunction with a mail hauberk or a leather coat.

In the final analysis, victory in the Battle of Barnet did not depend upon the quality of arms and armour. The heaving congealed mass

15th Century heavily armoured infantry with halberd (left) and lance with an early handgunner. GEOFFREY WHEELER

of humanity, pounding with sword, axe, club and gauntleted fist, assumed a monstrous existence of its own as individuality was submerged in a common struggle for survival. Shifting back and forth, constantly giving and taking ground, this homogenous expression of brute force seemed bent on self-destruction. It favoured no man, with combatants stumbling over fallen foe and comrade alike. And yet the whole remained sensitive to the behaviour of its component parts. The fear experienced by a single man was transmitted to a nerve centre, through which others became infected. As the virus spread, and one half of the mass weakened, so the other half grew in strength until the weaker was engulfed in a tidal wave of unbridled aggression.

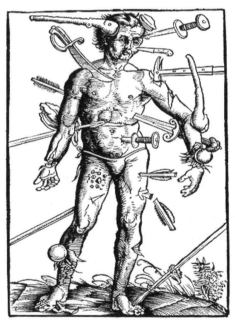

Above: Diagram of the type of wounds that the surgeon could expect to deal with following an edged weapons and early firearms battle.

Left: Scale model of Milanese field armour c1450 on the effigy of Richard Beuchamp Earl of Warwick in St Mary's Church, Warwick, by Peter Rowe. GEOFFREY WHEELER

Helm from Melbury Sampford, Dorset. GEOFFREY WHEELER

Helmet from Stourton Church, Wilts. GEOFFREY WHEELER

Coventry sallet. GEOFFREY WHEELER

Sallet, Royal Armouries GEOFFREY WHEELER

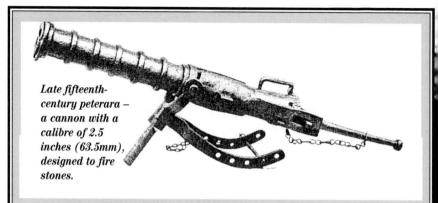

Late fifteenth-century peterara – a cannon with a calibre of 2.5 inches (63.5mm), designed to fire stones.

Firearms

Richard Brooke's *Visits to Fields of Battle in England of the Fifteenth Century* (1857) includes a chapter on the use of firearms by the English in the fifteenth century. The author seeks to put to rest the erroneous concept that 'cannon and other firearms' were not generally used by English armies until the following century.

In support of his argument, Brooke cites many instances of the use of guns during the Wars of the Roses. At the First Battle of St Albans (1455), the Yorkists were assembled 'with grete multitude of people harneised, and other abillements of werre, as gonnes and other'. At Ludford (1459) the Yorkists 'traiterously raunged in bataill, fortefied their chosen ground, their cartes with gonnes sette before their batailles ... and than and there shotte their seid gonnes'. At the Battle of Northampton (1460) 'the King's ordinance of guns might not be shot, there was so great raine that day'. At Empingham (1469) Edward IV 'set on the Lincolnshir men, and sparkelid them with his ordinaunce'. At Barnet (1471) Edward had 'three hundred of Flemmynges with hande-gonnes' while, before the battle, he and Warwick 'shotte gunnes at night one at the other'. At Tewkesbury (1471) both Yorkists and Lancastrians were well furnished with 'great artillerie'. At Bosworth (1485), according to Philip de Commines, Henry Tudor had 'quelques pieces d'artillerie', Richard III also fielding a number of 'gunnes'. At Stoke Field (1487) the Yorkists were armed with 'swerdys, speris, marespikes, bowes, gonnes, harneys, brigandynes, hawberkes, and many other wepyns'.

The list is quite impressive, but Brooke's *prima facie* case requires some qualification. Although guns, both large and small, were often to be found on fifteenth-century English battlefields, they rarely influenced the outcome of a battle. An exception is the Battle of Empingham, where the Yorkist artillery put the rebel Lancastrians to flight – probably without inflicting any serious harm. At the First Battle of St Albans the handguns of Warwick's Burgundians blew up in their faces. At Barnet, Warwick's night-long artillery barrage failed to do any damage, while Edward's Flemish handgunners apparently achieved little. The main practical value of artillery at this time lay in siege warfare, when time could be taken to site and aim a heavy gun. Thus cannon were present at the sieges of Alnwick, Bamburgh and Dunstanburgh Castles in 1463 and at the siege of Hornby Castle in 1471.

In addition, none of the guns in use during the Wars of the Roses were home-grown. The first English cannon foundry was not established until 1521, and during the Wars of the Roses all guns had to be imported, often together with foreign mercenaries trained in their use. Despite a reluctance to sponsor innovation, however, English governments did appear to recognize the future importance of firepower, and Edward IV took care to appoint a 'Master of Ordnance'.

Fifteenth-century field artillery could not challenge the supremacy of the medieval archer, and the practice of archery was enforced in both England and Scotland.
GEOFFREY WHEELER

Additional hooks and spikes incorporated into many fifteenth-century infantry weapons resulted in such horrific wounds that efforts were made to ban their use.
GEOFFREY WHEELER

Chapter Ten

MODERN INTERPRETATIONS OF
THE BATTLE OF BARNET

TO THE MAN IN THE STREET (insofar as such a creature existed in the fifteenth century) the Battle of Barnet remained a closed book. At the end of the day, the winner was Edward; that was all people needed to know. Even rank and file participants would have been unable to give an overview of the fight itself. Surviving soldiers may have returned home with tales of individual exploits, which over the years would fade into oblivion. Occasionally the chroniclers might rescue an embellished story or two, in an effort to piece together a coherent narrative, but much of their writing was based upon hearsay and conjecture. The task facing modern historians, whose accounts of the battle are necessarily based upon these unreliable primary sources, is nothing short of monumental.

The eminently readable C.V. Wedgwood, whose speciality was the seventeenth century (*The King's Peace The King's War*), also produced accounts of a number of British battles. Her version of Barnet is typically graphic, as demonstrated by her reference to the action as 'a series of groping miscalculations' – a rich phrase capturing the sense of confusion created by the fog and the mischance which attended Oxford's return to the battlefield. Warwick, described as 'usually being old-fashioned enough' to fight mounted, chooses to fight on foot so as not to appear inferior to Edward. Overtaken and despatched while 'running to Wrotham Park where he had left his horse', the Kingmaker is dismissed as 'the greatest and meanest troublemaker in the history of England'.

Churchill, in his mammoth *A History of the English-Speaking Peoples*, also suggests that 'imputations upon his physical courage' may have stung Warwick into fighting on foot. The author's own celebrated gift for an apt turn of phrase is apparent in the observation: 'Throughout England no one could see clearly what was happening, and the Battle of Barnet, which resolved their doubts, was itself fought in a fog.' While admitting that Warwick had received 'ill-usage from the youth he had placed and sustained upon the throne', Churchill argues that he had earned his grisly end through his 'depraved abandonment of all the causes for which he had sent so many men to their doom'.

Of course, the historian whose brief it is to provide a textbook covering a century or more of English political and social life can do little more than make a passing reference to battles. Thus E.F. Jacob in his volume in the Oxford History of England series, *The Fifteenth Century 1388–1485*, gives a succinct account of the Battle of Barnet, but concludes with the doubtful proposition regarding Warwick's death: 'A messenger sent by Edward IV from his own household was just too late to prevent the deed.'

General battlefield guides are, of necessity, brimful of generalizations. However, in his volume *British Battlefields: The South*, Philip Warner provides a refreshingly bold account of the battle. Interestingly, he points out that there is no proof of the generally accepted view that the lines of battle overlapped, adding that it was simply 'a tendency for armies before the days of good maps and binoculars to swing to the right.' Therefore Gloucester's assault upon Exeter naturally took the form of an outflanking manoeuvre, as did Oxford's advance upon Hastings' position. Warner goes on to suggest that Warwick, far from being foolhardy in fighting on foot, was cautious in having his mount in readiness, albeit well to the rear. In support of his argument, Warner relates the story that at Ferrybridge, in order to demonstrate his commitment, Warwick had killed his horse in full view of his men.

The Earl of Warwick prepares to meet Edward IV in battle. "Warwick this day must take the same risks as the commonest soldier in the field and remain on foot."
BASED ON A TABLEAU AT WARWICK CASTLE

The most unusual interpretation of the deployment of both armies is provided by Sir James Ramsay in *Lancaster and York*. According to Ramsay, the Lancastrians were strung out along the

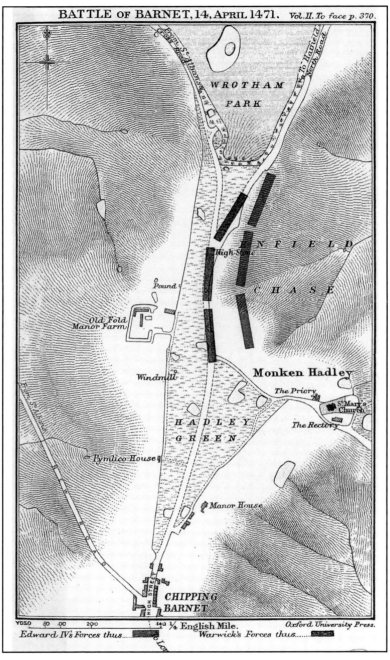

Sir James Ramsay's interpretation of the Battle of Barnet.

Great North Road between Wrotham Park and Monken Hadley Green, from which position they 'could take the King's troops in detail as they came out of the narrow street of Barnet'. Edward took his men 'in the dark along the low ground to the East of the high road, so as to avoid debouching from the town in face of the enemy, and to get his men safely deployed for a fair attack all along the line'.

A sober assessment is made by John Effingham in his *The Wars of the Roses*. In his view, the fog 'which made it so hard for the combatants to see one another makes it easier for the historian ... to see the unfolding pattern of the battle.' According to Effingham, the fact that the Lancastrian left wing did not collapse worked to Edward's advantage, for Gloucester was not drawn from the field as was Oxford. Instead, Exeter's battle was merely rolled back, Gloucester's advance giving 'additional impetus to the king's own thrust in the centre'. Following the *Arrivall's* account very closely, Effingham ascribes the Yorkist victory to Edward's personal contribution. The incident of Oxford's return and the confusion between the badges – emanating from Warkworth's account – is described as 'doubtful', one of several 'personal touches and vivid anecdotes' added for effect in later years. Such an assessment makes no allowance for the *Arrivall's* unashamedly Yorkist sympathies. Again, given the poor visibility any similarity between badges was bound to lead to confusion and muddle.

Effingham also states that the fog must have meant that those fighting on the wings of both armies remained unaware of events. Richard Brooke in *Visits to Fields of Battle in England of the Fifteenth Century* draws the same inference. Oxford 'broke a part of the ranks of the Yorkists, and several of the fugitives fled to London, and gave out that the Lancastrians were victorious. This, however, proved to be of no eventual advantage, and gave no encouragement to the other forces of Warwick, because the fog prevented their being fully aware of it.' Brooke claims that Warwick fought 'at the head of his troops' and, unlike Wedgwood, sees him as a 'great, valiant and powerful' individual.

In his *Battles and Battlefields of England* C.R.B. Barrett remarks upon the 'curious composition' of the line of battle: 'Men who a dozen times had been ranged against each other, who had in cold blood executed one another's relatives, sacked one another's castles and houses, and ravaged one another's manors and estates, were now fighting side by side, and it must be admitted not without considerable suspicions of the fidelity of one another.' Such distrust

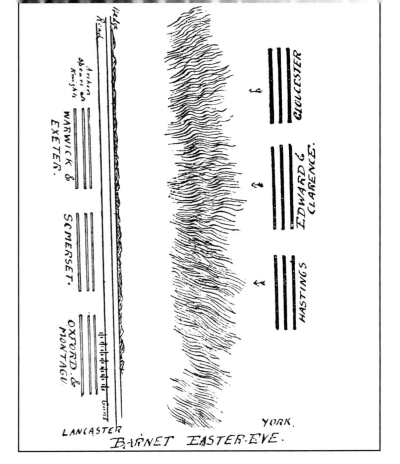

C.R.B. Barrett's interpretation of the Yorkist and Lancastrian deployment at the Battle of Barnet.

undoubtedly had an influence on the result of the battle. Barrett does query the likelihood of participants confusing the badges of Edward and Oxford. In truth, the *rose-en-soleil* of Edward and the *mullet argent* of Oxford are by no means identical, but the rose would certainly have been of a simpler nature than those depicted in heraldic texts and, as Barrett says, 'that it could have been mistaken in a fog for the mullet argent seems more than probable.'

Another problem with which Barrett struggles somewhat is the question of deployment, for in this matter he appears to follow Ramsay. If Ramsay is correct in his selection of a north-south axis for the battle lines, then how could the outflanked Hastings have fled in the direction of Barnet? As Barrett states: 'Their obvious direction of flight would have been to the north-east, down the hill, and then by a circuitous road southwards.' A similar argument

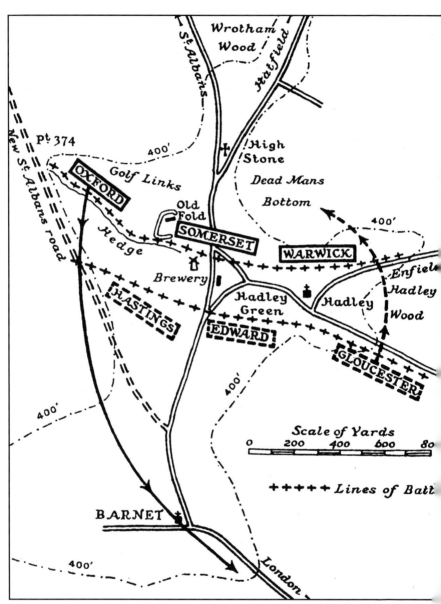

Alfred Burne's plan of the Battle of Barnet, showing the Lancastrian right wing extending to St Albans Road.

applies to the route of Oxford's return to the battlefield. On the other hand, the mention of hedges might lend weight to Ramsay. Barrett suggests that 'hedges were infrequent in those days, and many years afterwards were the reverse of common. But such a boundary might with considerable probability have fringed the road.'

In *Battles in Britain 1066-1547*, William Seymour suggests that Warwick was 'in command of a small reserve behind the centre'. Like Brooke and Effingham, he is an admirer of Warwick, averring that 'the story of this man enshrines all the chivalrous romanticism of the Middle Ages. He was not only immensely popular with the masses, but he made a deeper and more lasting impression on his own century than any other man who was not a prince of the blood.' Seymour's account does illustrate the importance of cultivating a personal acquaintance with the battlefield, which, he states, 'even now holds a good deal of water'.

As John Kinross (*The Battlefields of Britain*) has indicated, there are similarities between Barnet and the English Civil War battle of Marston Moor (1644). At Marston Moor, Cromwell and Leslie smashed the Royalist right wing while Goring inflicted severe

In Battles in Britain 1066-1547, William Seymour suggests that Warwick was 'in command of a small reserve behind the centre'.

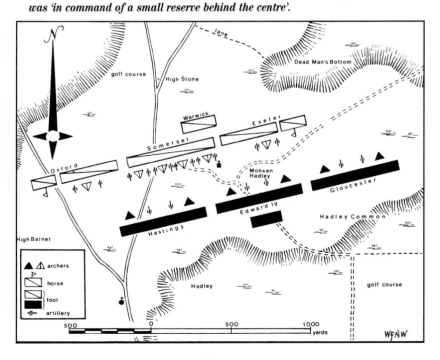

115

damage upon the Roundhead right. The battle was fought along a comparatively wide front of almost two miles (3.2km) so that the events unfolding at one end of the battlefield were initially a mystery to combatants on the other flank. At one point, assuming all was lost, the Roundhead generals Leven, Manchester and Fairfax all fled the field, bearing the premature and erroneous news that the Royalists had won a famous victory.

Again, at the Battle of Naseby (1645), where the battlefield was more compact, Prince Rupert broke Ireton's Roundhead cavalry and chased them from the field, Rupert's men then loitering to sack the Roundhead baggage train in much the same way as Oxford's men tarried to plunder Barnet. However, the Battle of Naseby took place in broad daylight, and although the rest of the Roundhead army was well aware that their left wing had been destroyed they fought on to victory.

The battlefield at Barnet was also quite limited in extent, with the divisions tightly packed. Despite the fog, the Yorkist centre could well have been aware of the disaster taking place to its left, and yet, if so, this did not deter it from fighting on. In fact the Yorkists may have been spurred on to greater efforts. In the same way that a football team is at its most vulnerable in the immediate aftermath of scoring a goal, Oxford's initial success may have caused the Lancastrian centre to relax, providing the shrewd Edward with an ideal opportunity to launch an effective counter-attack.

One of the most influential of modern accounts is that provided by Alfred Burne in *The Battlefields of England*. Burne dismisses Ramsay's proposed site as 'preposterous', which is a little unfair for, although unlikely, it remains a possibility. As our knowledge of the battle is dependent upon conflicting partisan accounts compiled some years after the event, one cannot afford to be too scathing about the other fellow's theories. In fact, Ramsay's suggested deployment would not be amiss in terms of the second phase of the battle, when the Lancastrian right flank and the Yorkist left had been turned.

In Burne's version, Somerset is in command of the Lancastrian centre and Warwick, at 44 years of age, is at 'the height of his natural powers'. (With average life expectancy standing at 40 years, Warwick was actually living on borrowed time.) Burne also has Edward mounted on a white charger. If this were so, then Warwick must have regretted choosing to fight on foot so as not to lose face.

In *Warwick the Kingmaker*, Paul Murray Kendall expands the

story in which Montagu urges his brother to give up his horse: 'The Marquess drew him apart from their household knights and squires. Men's minds were uneasy, John Neville told his brother. To give them heart, Warwick this day must take the same risks as the commonest soldier in the field and remain on foot... . Warwick agreed to his brother's demand.' Maintaining a fine balance between historical accuracy and readability, Kendall lauds Warwick's generalship:

> Warwick and his lieutenants struggled to bolster the wavering ranks. But before the Earl could restore order, Edward smashed with all his remaining reserve at the heart of the Lancastrian centre. The great sun banner drove towards Montagu's pennon. Warwick called on the last of his reserve. He thrust up his visor to hearten them with cheering words, to urge stragglers back into the battle – if they held now, victory was theirs!

For the ultimate in heroic prose one need look no further than Caroline Halsted's *Richard III*:

> No battle in our warlike annals was more terrible, more characterised by the worst passions of humanity, than that which in this year marked a festival peculiarly consecrated throughout the Christian world, to advocating the heavenly doctrines of the holy Founder of

Some accounts have Warwick starting the battle on horseback and finishing it on foot. Figure of Warwick 'The Kingmaker' by the Armoury of St James.
GEOFFREY WHEELER

117

our religion, and designed to commemorate 'on earth peace, good-will towards men.' No hosannas ushered in the dawn of this most holy day; but on the contrary, vows of extermination, of hatred, of revenge.

Halsted has Warwick starting the battle on horseback and finishing it on foot – a suggestion which is not without merit:

The Earl of Warwick, after a time, dismounted, and fought on foot. He urged on his followers with the determination of his character, and with all the energy of desperation; but in vain. Surrounded by his enemies, and prevented by a thick mist from discerning the situation of his friends, he fell – a victim to his misplaced zeal, to his ungovernable pride and fatal ambition.

The battle of Barnet, 1471, from a French version of the official Yorkist chronicle of the campaign sent Edward IV to Charles the Bold

Although inaccurate (note the castle in the background), this is the only known contemporary illustration of the Battle of Barnet.

In *Medieval English Warfare*, R.R. Sellman makes an obvious but often overlooked point in connection with Warwick's demise: 'His death, rather than the victory itself, made this action decisive.' Had Warwick effected an escape, and succeeded in joining Queen Margaret's army, his presence would have been instrumental in attracting additional support.

When all is said and done, one is left with the inescapable conclusion that all that can be said about the Battle of Barnet with absolute certainty is that it was fought near Barnet, that the Yorkists won, and that the Earl of Warwick was killed.

The Wars of the Roses: A Marxist Interpretation

In his classic textbook *A People's History of England*, the Marxist historian A.L. Morton sees the Wars of the Roses as an expression of a class struggle in which the English nobility self-destructed. In the aftermath of the Hundred Years' War, he argues, with nobles looking around for new ways to enrich themselves, coupled with the existence of bands of demobilized soldiers roaming the land, 'a general outbreak of civil war was inevitable'.

London merchants prospered under Edward IV, winning bans on the importation of everything from cutlery and hardware to playing cards and tennis balls.

Medieval street scene. It has often been argued that much of England remained untouched by the Wars of the Roses, with the routine of town and country activity continuing as in times of peace.

The exploitation of a weak monarchy, personified in *Henry VI*, by a politically ambitious nobility certainly fits Morton's hypothesis. This elite, whether it be Yorkist or Lancastrian, sought to profit at the expense of the taxpayer as more and more money from royal revenues was siphoned off into a few private purses. It might be argued that the Wars of the Roses themselves were fought more for profit than out of any high-minded allegiance to the Houses of York and Lancaster – hence the significance of the Acts of Attainder through which sequestered estates were redistributed, and the readiness with which supporters changed sides.

Lancastrian support tended to come from the feudal backwaters of the North and West, while Yorkist support was more bourgeois, focusing on the South and the merchant class in general. Edward IV made an effort to maintain good relations with the merchants both at home and abroad. In particular he cultivated the friendship of the Hanse towns, for he was well aware of their influence in terms of maritime

Medieval agricultural labourers. While the merchant classes prospered under Edward IV, the arduous life of the land worker remained largely unchanged.

affairs, having used Hanse ships to effect his landing at Ravenspur in March 1472. In fact the Hanse traders secured preferential treatment, and in 1473 were authorised to pay less in customs duties.

The Earl of Warwick was chief among the old guard of nobles who sought to maintain the status quo by challenging Edward at the Battle of Barnet. Another opportunity presented itself on Edward's death, when the survivors made a last ditch attempt to maintain their position by supporting Gloucester in his bid for power. They soon found, to their cost, that Richard III had no intention of sharing anything, and they transferred their allegiance to Henry Tudor. Again they were destined to suffer disappointment as, to quote Morton, the new monarchy 'was of a totally new kind, based upon a new relation of class forces'.

Medieval Hanse coat of arms.

Further Reading

Ashdown, Charles Henry. *European Arms & Armour*, Brussel & Brussel, 1967.

Baldwin, David. *Elizabeth Woodville: Mother of the Princes in the Tower*, Sutton Publishing, 2002.

Barrett, C.R.B. *Battles and Battlefields in England*, Innes, 1896.

Boardman, Andrew W. *The Medieval Soldier in the Wars of the Roses*, Sutton Publishing, 1998.

Brooke, Richard. *Visits to Fields of Battle in England of the Fifteenth Century*, John Russell Smith, 1857.

Burne, Alfred H. *The Battlefields of England*, Methuen, 1950.

Cass, Frederick. *The Battle of Barnet*, London & Middlesex Archaeological Society, 1882.

Churchill, Winston S. *A History of the English Speaking Peoples: The Birth of Britain*, Cassell & Co, 1956.

Dockray, Keith. *Edward IV: A Source Book*, Sutton Publishing, 1999.

Dockray, Keith. *Henry VI, Margaret of Anjou and the Wars of the Roses*, Sutton Publishing, 2000.

Effingham, John. *The Wars of the Roses: Peace and Conflict in Fifteenth-Century England*, Weidenfeld and Nicolson, 1981.

FitzRoy, Charles & Harry, Keith (eds). *Grafton Regis: The History of a Northamptonshire Village*, Merton Priory Press, 2000.

Gelder, W.H. *Monken Hadley Church and Village*, Falkland Press, 1986.

Goodman, Anthony. *The Wars of the Roses: The Soldiers' Experience*, Tempus Publishing, 2005.

Haigh, Philip A. *The Wars of the Roses: From Wakefield to Towton*, Leo Cooper, 2002.

Halsted, Caroline A. *Richard III: As Duke of Gloucester and King of England, Volume I*, Longman, Brown, Green and Longmans, 1844.

Hammond, P.W. *The Battles of Barnet and Tewkesbury*, Sutton Publishing, 1990.

Hicks, Michael. *False, Fleeting, Perjur'd Clarence: George, Duke of Clarence 1449–78*, Sutton Publishing, 1980.

Jacob, E.F. *The Fifteenth Century: 1399–1485*, Oxford University Press, 1961.

Jones, Fiona. *The Battle of Barnet*, Barnet & District Local History Society, 2004.

Kendall, Paul Murray. *Warwick the Kingmaker*, George Allen & Unwin, 1957.

Kinross, John. *The Battlefields of Britain*, David & Charles, 1979.

McGill, Patrick. *The Battle of Barnet 1471*, Freezywater Publications, 1996.

Morton, A.L. *A People's History of England*, Lawrence & Wishart, 1965.

Oman, Sir Charles. *A History of the Art of War in the Middle Ages, Volume II*, Methuen, 1924.

Oman, Sir Charles. *Warwick the Kingmaker*, Macmillan, 1905.

Pollard, Tony & Oliver, Neil. *Two Men in a Trench*, Michael Joseph, 2002.

Ramsay, Sir James H. *Lancaster and York: A Century of English History (AD 1399–1485), Volume II*, Clarendon Press, 1892.

Ross, Charles. *The Wars of the Roses*, Thames and Hudson, 1976.

Sellman, R.R. *Medieval English Warfare*, Methuen, 1960.

Seymour, William. *Battles in Britain Volume I, 1066–1547*, Sidgwick & Jackson, 1975.

Smurthwaite, David. *The Ordnance Survey Complete Guide to the Battlefields of Britain*, Webb & Bower, 1984.

Virgoe, Roger (ed). *Illustrated letters of the Paston Family*, Macmillan, 1989.

Visser-Fuchs, Livia. 'A Ricardian Riddle: the Casualty List of the Battle of Barnet', *The Ricardian* VIII, 1988.

Warner, Philip. *British Battlefields: The South*, Osprey Publishing, 1972.

Warrington, John (ed). *The Paston Letters, Volume II*, Dent, 1956.

Wars of the Roses DVD in Cromwell Productions' 'History of Warfare' series. For details see their website: www.pegasus-records.com.

Wedgwood, C.V. *Battlefields in Britain*, Collins, 1944.

Further Information

Barnet Museum (pictured below) is situated at 30 Wood Street, Barnet EN5 4BE (Tel: 020 8440 8066).
Opening hours:
Tuesday–Thursday 2.30–4.30pm, Saturday 10.30am–12.30pm and 2.00pm–4.00pm.

The Richard III Society promotes research into the life of Richard III, although its remit extends to the Wars of the Roses in general. Also publishes a respected journal, *The Ricardian*. Website: www.richardiii.net.

The Battlefields Trust is dedicated to the preservation, interpretation and presentation of battlefields as educational and heritage resources. Website: www.battlefieldstrust.com.

The Wars of the Roses website provides well-presented background information about the conflict. Website: www.warsoftheroses.com.

The Fifteenth Century website includes links to a number of fifteenth-century battle re-enactment society sites. Website: www.fifteenthcentury.net.

The Barnet Times occasionally runs articles on matters of interest relating to the Battle of Barnet. Website: www.barnettimes.co.uk.

INDEX